*Plans for Political Reform*
*in Imperial Russia, 1730-1905*

*Russian Civilization Series*

*Editors*

MICHAEL CHERNIAVSKY
IVO J. LEDERER

# Plans for Political Reform
# in Imperial Russia, 1730-1905

MARC RAEFF
*Columbia University*

PRENTICE-HALL, INC., *Englewood Cliffs, New Jersey*

Prentice-Hall International, Inc., *London*
Prentice-Hall of Australia, Pty. Ltd., *Sydney*
Prentice-Hall of Canada, Ltd., *Toronto*
Prentice-Hall of India (Private) Ltd., *New Delhi*
Prentice-Hall of Japan, Inc., *Tokyo*

Current printing (last digit):
10   9   8   7   6   5   4   3   2   1

Library of Congress Catalog Card No.: 66-11189
Printed in the United States of America
C-67940 (P)      C-67941 (C)

# Foreword to the Series

————◀◉▶————

The presentation of Russian history and civilization in this country has been shaped to a significant extent by the absence of adequate original source materials. Linguistic competence in Russian remains today indispensable for advanced training and research. It is regrettable, however, that the majority of students interested in Russia but not in command of the language should be denied opportunities for delving into the raw materials of Russian history.

Our purpose is thus relatively simple: to make widely available important Russian sources and to help remove Russian studies from the realm of the arcane and the exotic. Each volume in the series is designed to present source material on a significant problem of a given period—medieval, Imperial, or Soviet. Each volume, moreover, involves a careful translation and basic annotation so as to be intelligible to the undergraduate or the general reader and of scholarly use to the graduate student, to teachers, and to non-Russian specialists.

The series, spanning both the Tsarist and Soviet eras, concentrates on hitherto untranslated sources. In the main, too, it presents them in full text and without abridgment so as to expose both flavor and meaning in a document, memoir, or treatise. In this the series deliberately differs from the documentary collections usually found in one-volume compendia covering long periods and many themes.

The introductory essay in each volume places the issues and sources in their larger context. The essays are designed to provide guidance to the reader and generate new approaches to the understanding of the distant and recent Russian past.

*Michael Cherniavsky*
*Ivo J. Lederer*

# *Preface*

◆

The projects presented in this book have been selected from among a much larger number of plans available for two basic reasons: (1) they were relatively well known in Russia and, therefore, could be assumed to have had an impact on the thinking of officials and leaders of public opinion, and (2) they are relatively compact and clear. In the 18th and early 19th centuries men wrote at inordinate length, and not too clearly; many projects and proposals for reform could not be used here because they were too long and full of confusing and unclear technical detail. It was felt that documents dealing with general political problems, rather than with institutional and organizational details, would be more meaningful and useful for an understanding of Russian political thinking.

The translations have been made from the most complete and authoritative versions available. The dates are those of the original, i.e., according to the Julian calendar in use in Russia until 1918, which lagged behind the Gregorian calendar by eleven days in the 18th century, twelve days in the 19th century, and thirteen days in the 20th century. The following symbols occur in the text:

...          omission by editor
[ ]          insertion by editor
( )          parentheses in original
// //        summary or paraphrase by editor
/ /          additions or earlier wording in the original

The abbreviation PSZ is used in the text and notes for *Polnoe Sobranie Zakonov Rossiiskoi Imperii* (Complete Collection of the Laws of the Russian Empire), 1st series, St. Petersburg, 1833.

I wish to thank the Russian Institute of Columbia University for technical assistance and Prentice-Hall for editorial supervision and advice.

*Marc Raeff*

# Contents

*ix*

# IV

*Project for a Most Graciously Granted Charter
to the Russian People (1801)*

# V

*Principles of Government Reform
(of the Unofficial Committee, 1802)*

# VI

*Introduction to the Codification of State
Laws by M. M. Speransky (1809)*

# VII

*N. N. Novosil'tsev: Constitutional Charter of
the Russian Empire (1818-1820)*

# VIII

*Memorandum of State Secretary Valuev
(13 April 1863)*

# IX

*Memorandum Submitted to the Emperor by the
Minister of the Interior, Count M. T.
Loris-Melikov (28 January 1881)*

# X

*All-Highest Manifesto on the Establishment
of a State Duma*

*Bibliography*

*Plans for Political Reform
in Imperial Russia, 1730-1905*

# Introduction

As a nation or society undergoes change, its institutions, too, have to be transformed to adjust to new conditions and needs. Failing this, there develop strains and stresses which, if allowed to go on, may result in the sudden and violent upheavals we call revolutions. As a society and polity, Russia was launched onto the path of rapid and extensive transformations by Peter the Great. Of course, there had been change before Peter, but such transformations had been very gradual and limited in scope. Since Peter's times the elite, at any rate, had endeavored to make Russia the equal of the Western European states and to have it participate actively in what we call modern Western civilization. Yet some of Russia's basic institutions failed to adjust adequately to the new orientation, to the urge for change. Hence the strains and stresses that eventually led to the collapse of Imperial Russia, a collapse that took place in two stages—in 1905 and 1917.

Naturally, the process of inadequate adjustment and ultimate breakdown did not go unchallenged. At various times efforts were made by individuals or groups to bring about reforms to decrease the strains on the Russian polity and exorcise the threat of upheaval and revolution. These efforts were directed at a variety of institutions and conditions that needed correction: serfdom and then the agrarian crisis, administration and justice, education and cultural life. Throughout the entire period, however, the condition and nature of the state was the center of attention; it was the one institution that influenced, if it did not actually dictate and create, all the other conditions that needed correction. Furthermore, the Russian state, whatever its weaknesses, retained to the last the power to assist or prevent the realization of the proposals and reforms that were advanced. Naturally, therefore, the state itself ultimately became the principal object of reform proposals.

The extremely powerful and influential Russian state was an autocracy. Any reform had perforce to aim at the very center of the institution, that is, the position and role of the autocrat and those organs of government directly associated with him. All other government institutions, whatever their direct impact on the population, were always, and quite correctly, seen as reflections of the central organs in St. Petersburg. The thoughtful Russian was convinced (and historical experience validated his belief) that no partial or local reform had much chance of success without some radical change in the attitudes and practices of the central authorities as well. For this reason, the most important projects of general political reform were concerned primarily with the central governmental institutions in St. Petersburg and the role of autocracy. It is this circumstance which determined our consideration here of only those projects of reform that dealt with the central institutions of the Empire.

From the death of Peter the Great to about 1825, the members of Russia's educated elite remained basically loyal to the system created by the first Emperor. This was not true, of course, of the common people, whose revolts were directed as much against the Petrine system as against individual landlords or specific abuses. After 1825 the situation changed, and there developed among the upper classes widespread and vociferous opposition to the very principles of the Russian polity. Many of these opponents of the regime advocated extensive changes aimed at creating a new society as well as another political system. Yet there were also many who believed and hoped that the political structure might be reformed from inside, without provoking sharp breaks and violent social upheavals whose ultimate consequences could not be foreseen. Members of the Establishment itself frequently and insistently clamored for reform in the basic structure of Russia's political and administrative institutions in order to forestall revolutionary upheavals.

The programs of revolutionary groups were directed to the future, when the imperial regime would be a thing of the past. The reform proposals, on the other hand, were directed to the present; they were, therefore, of more immediate relevance in determining the country's development. Their failure proved as important as the revolutionary movements themselves in bringing about the collapse of the regime.

Whatever their roots in the past of Muscovy, the reforms of Peter the Great marked the beginning of a new era in Russia's public life. It is hardly an exaggeration to speak of Peter the Great as the founder of the modern Russian state who set the framework of its institutional development for the entire course of the eighteenth and nineteenth centuries. Obviously, Peter did not build on empty ground; the very nature of Russia's past and the characteristic features of Muscovite society enabled the first Emperor to give a radically novel form to the institutional pattern, but at the same time imposed limitations on their later development.

Muscovy had evolved a pattern of institutional and political life that clearly distinguished it from both Eastern and Western medieval traditions and practices. Disregarding many qualifications of detail, we might say that the Muscovite polity had displayed the following basic traits since the middle of the sixteenth century: First, the power of the Tsar over all his subjects and all facets of national life was absolute and virtually unchallenged. All policy decisions of any consequence were made only by the Tsar, with the assistance of his close advisers. Second, and, of course, deriving from the first, was the virtual absence of corporations and political or social estates, and thus the extreme insecurity and limited rights which characterized even the so-called privileged classes. Of course, in view of the vastness of the realm and the limited technological means at the disposal of the government in the sixteenth and seventeenth centuries, Moscow could not take over all functions of local administration. Although a trend toward restricting local administrative and judicial autonomies had become manifest since the end of the Times of Troubles in the early seventeenth century, it had not yet eliminated some elective local institutions, more particularly in the north-eastern regions of the realm. Moreover, Moscow interfered little in the daily routine of villages and peasant communes.

Although exalted to nearly divine status and surrounded by a complicated ceremonial of Byzantine origin which set him off from common mortals, the Tsar manifested his power in essentially patriarchal forms. The Tsardom of Muscovy was considered the patrimony (*votchina*) of the Tsar, and its inhabitants were entrusted to his paternal care. In other words, political authority was still expressed very much in personal terms: in all important matters, and even in many trifling ones, the Tsar's personal command was final, and it was to the Tsar himself that his subjects always turned in case of need. Officials of the government were viewed only as the personal representatives of the ruler; in the performance of their duties they merely carried out the "errands" (*posylka*) of the Tsar; they were his "servants" (*kholop*) and had no authority of their own. In principle, at least, their actions were based on tradition and custom, and the Tsar was the guardian of these hallowed practices. Of course, this was the theory; the practice was departing from it increasingly. Yet even in their breach the old theory and tradition continued to play a considerable role. In the mind of the seventeenth-century Russian, whether nobleman or peasant, the Tsar's personal concern and actions helped to temper the harshness of his rule. Nor should we forget the essential fact that the function of government was conceived largely in negative terms. The Tsar was the protector of his people: defender against external enemies, guardian of the Orthodox faith and of those principles and customs which made for the good life of his God-fearing subjects. He was the just ruler who righted wrongs, succored the poor and orphaned, and by his own exemplary life and deeds helped to maintain his Orthodox Christian people in the grace of God. It was the typical medieval Christian view of kingship, and if in Moscow such an outlook did not conflict with the fact that the government played an active role in certain areas of public life (especially the economic), it was due to the weakness of the estate structure and the absence of autonomous centers of power.

Some of these characteristic features of Muscovite society had been modified in the course of the seventeenth century, and new elements had come to the fore. The expansion of the territory, increasingly more frequent and extensive military and commercial involvements with Western Europe, and the growing complexity of national life had all contributed to a decline of the patrimonial, functionally undifferentiated character of government. We note the government's growing concern with matters which heretofore had been outside its ken, such as the establishment of industrial enterprises and various new cultural activities, including theaters and schools. The continuing process of centralization and functional organization of the administration weakened further the already feeble elements of regional and group solidarity and loyalty. Finally, the roles of tradition and birthright were waning, as illustrated by the rise of professional army units, the abolition of the *mestnichestvo,* the disappearance of the *Zemskii Sobor,* and the decline of the *Boiar Duma.*

In spite of these changes, the basic structure and character of Muscovite public life remained almost unaffected, because the transformations occurred very gradually, without bringing radical innovations into existing institutions and relationships. Moreover, these transformations were barely perceptible to the contemporary observer; their potential contribution to the shaping of a new society was not realized. Most important of all, there had been no break in the continuity of Russian culture and no consciousness, therefore, of being confronted by an alien spirit and a new system of values. Thus, the subjects of Tsar Theodore had no reason to feel or believe that their situation was in any appreciable way different from that of their grandparents in the reign of Michael. Into this unawareness burst Peter the Great, with his ruthless energy and seemingly revolutionary program of innovation. Historians who, like S. Platonov, have stressed the basic continuity of Russian history and played down the revolutionary impact of

Peter's reforms have underestimated this aspect of the situation.[1]
Fastening only on the apparent formal or technical similarity in
Russian institutions before and after Peter, these historians have
concluded that the first Emperor did not really innovate much.
But the fact remains—and in itself it is of historical significance—
that contemporaries disregarded these similarities and were primarily conscious of having experienced a radical break, and it is this
awareness of a change that they transmitted to their children and
children's children.

It is possible, for our purposes, to disregard the complicated
structural detail of Peter's institutions, as well as the twists and
turns of his legislation. We may summarize the eventual results of
his reforms as follows: The ruler's person was separated from the
government; henceforth the ruler viewed himself, and came to be
considered by many of his subjects, as the servant of the interests and
welfare of the *state*—a new concept, which in reality covered a
congeries of institutions. The areas of governmental concern were
extended to cover nearly all aspects of national life and many
phases of personal life. Through its administrative institutions and
its officials the state frequently took the initiative in establishing
and promoting new fields of public and private endeavor, so that
for several generations it became the principal industrial and commercial entrepreneur, the chief educator, and even a leader in the
country's cultural and social life. Such an extension of governmental
concern led to the creation of many new administrative and cultural institutions of all types, a tremendous increase in the number
of government officials, and the elaboration of rules to guide the
actions of both institutions and officials. These rules were drafted
either in imitation of available Western European models or on
the basis of rational and theoretical considerations. There could
no longer be an appeal to tradition or old custom ("as done in
olden times"); the new rules could be justified only by appealing to
some abstract concept or value—hence the rationalist and univer-
salist character of Russian legislation in the eighteenth and early

[1] S. F. Platonov, *Lektsii po russkoi istorii*, I. Blinov, ed. (St. Petersburg:
1904), especially pp. 367-78 and 457-60; the same, "Boiarskaia duma—
predshestvennitsa Senata," *Stat'i po russkoi istorii (1883-1912)*, 2d ed. (St.
Petersburg: 1912), pp. 444-94.

nineteenth centuries. It is easy to see how the army could serve as the most readily available and most easily understood model for the civil administration to emulate, and it inspired not only Peter I, whose prime concerns during most of his reign were the needs of war, but his successors as well. The obvious danger was that form would outweigh content in administrative practice. Rationalist, abstract, formalistic legislation and administrative procedures tended to remove government from the realities of national life; it led officials to see their tasks in terms of shuffling papers and to forget the concrete human or particular local circumstances. Even after the appeal to rational concepts and foreign models (rather than to divine law and tradition) had lost its force in the course of the eighteenth century, the new administrative practices introduced by Peter could never build a bridge to the traditional political and moral consciousness of the common people.

The necessity of organizing new institutions and of adapting to "rational" (in Max Weber's sense) procedures and rules of administration put the ruling elite under great pressure. Throughout the first three quarters of the eighteenth century, policies and institutions were in constant flux, in search of a harmonious adaptation of the new norms to existing conditions and in search of stability in the face of frequent changes of rulers and favorites. This is why the codification of existing legislation became such a vital problem. Codification was necessary not only to eliminate laws reflecting outworn traditions and precedents but also to reconcile conflicting norms and procedures which *ad hoc* measures were constantly introducing. Not until the reign of Alexander I did the administrative organization initiated by Peter receive its more or less permanent shape, and not until Nicholas I was codification brought to a successful conclusion.

The main obstacle to a satisfactory adjustment of Peter's institutional innovations to Russian life was the nature of the people who staffed these institutions and acted according to the new rational principles of administration and legislation. In all fairness it must be said, though, that the barrier became an insuperable one largely because of the character of the society itself. At times one has the feeling that the gap between the Emperor's officials and his subjects was never bridged. No sooner had the officials learned how to deal with one type of problem than society's evolution had transformed their work and created new attitudes and forces which could not be solved by those very policies that, only recently, seemed to have been so successful. The lag between government and society was a result, as well as a cause, of the state's inability to bring about conditions of order and relative permanence which might have permitted social change without a radical transformation of the basic relationship between government and society. The fate which befell the projects of reform presented in this volume well illustrates this basic pattern.

The new administrative institutions created by Peter the Great and his immediate successors and the new legislation promulgated to direct the work of these institutions required officials capable of acting on the basis of formal, general, rational regulations within the framework of a highly organized bureaucratic hierarchy. This meant a radical departure from the more traditional and personal methods of earlier times. Essentially, the issue faced by the elite immediately after Peter's death (and in a way the problem remained a live one until the end of the imperial regime) was whether to follow the personal or the formal, bureaucratic approach in dealing with the population. It is quite striking to note how slowly the elements of personal relationship disappeared from Russian public life. Naturally, the very fact that the sovereign ruled as an absolute autocrat helped to perpetuate the personal element in government. Indeed, as long as appeal to the Emperor for his personal decision or judgment was possible, the exercise of political power retained something of its earlier patriarchal character, and the subordinate officials were seen, or considered themselves, as personal delegates of the monarch.[2] It was difficult to give up this view of authority. In the first place, there was a rather simple political and sociological reason: the personal appeal to

---

[2] Peter the Great himself contributed to the perpetuation of the personal element through the acts on single inheritance and on succession to the Russian throne. By these acts both the private landowner (also serf owner) and the ruling monarch were given the right to designate their successors and heirs freely, thereby strengthening the absolute patrimonial character of their authority. The acts in question are in PSZ, No. 3893 (5 February 1722, Statute on Succession to the Throne) and No. 2789 (23 March 1714, On Inheritance of Real and Movable Property).

the ruler or his delegate provided the only protection against or redress from injustice, abuse of power, or persecution by subordinate officials who acted on the basis of vague and poorly understood regulations. And it was easy for the officials to take advantage of the monarch's remoteness and of the ignorance, poverty, and weakness of those they were supposed to govern, but in fact oppressed. In addition, the sovereign was the embodiment of ethical and religious values, which remained powerful among the people and which at times found expression among the educated classes in times of public crisis or personal tragedy.[3] Of course, parallels to the personal character of political authority so nicely illustrated by Pushkin at the end of *The Captain's Daughter* could be found in the chronicles of all monarchies, but in Russia it retained greater force much longer, as witnessed, for example, in the behavior of many Decembrists or the aura which surrounded Alexander II.

With the westernization and modernization of the Russian state, such a personal relationship between rulers and ruled could not, of course, remain the foundation of administration and policy decisions. Bureaucratic norms and procedures had to be worked out, and, as always happens in such a case, they became the object of bitter resentment and hatred. Procedures seemed to have become mechanical, rules were frequently deemed arbitrary and injust, the attitudes of clerks and officials were felt to be callous or capricious. How could one secure "justice" (*pravda*) under such circumstances? And yet it was firmly believed by the people that the defense and enforcement of justice were the most important functions of political power.[4] Thus the officials, the bureaucracy, came to be seen as an insuperable barrier separating an understanding and compas-

---

[3] On the notions of true kingship in Russia see M. Cherniavsky, *Tsar and People—Studies in Russian Myths* (New Haven and London: Yale University Press, 1961).
[4] This view was also expressed by some influential and high-minded officials at the end of the eighteenth century. Cf. the memoirs of G. Derzhavin and Prince N. Lopukhin: *Zapiski Gavriila Romanovicha Derzhavina (1743-1812)* (Moscow: 1860); "Zapiski nekotorykh obstoiatel'stv zhizni i sluzhby d.t.s. senatora N. V. Lopukhina, sochinennye im samim," *Chteniia v imperatorskom obshchestve istorii i drevnostei rossiiskikh pri Moskovskom universitete* (1860), Bks. II and III.

sionate Tsar from his people. It is irrelevant in our context that
such a feeling might have been an illusion, a myth, or an unwar-
ranted, retrospective idealization of a relationship that had never
existed in this form even before Peter the Great. What matters is
the survival of the ideal and the expectation that authorities ought
to act in accordance with it. Paradoxically, perhaps, Nicholas I
tried in his own way to give practical and institutional form to this
political psychology. But the circumstances of Russian society had
changed, while the means Nicholas used (the Third Section of his
Chancellery and the Corps of Gendarmes) actually led to a contrary
result by giving yet greater scope to arbitrariness and corruption.[5]
The autocratic character of the Emperor's power contributed to
the survival of the belief that all things flowed from him and that
he could at any moment set all wrongs aright. This belief stayed
alive down to the Bloody Sunday of January, 1905, when it was
finally shattered in the minds of the common people as well. But
as long as it lived it bred a sense of frustration and grievance that
had its source in the dichotomy between personal (charismatic) and
rational (bureaucratic) norms of political action. This in itself did
not make the task of government and administration easy, even
had the institutions themselves been more workable and the officials more efficient.

The conflict between personal and bureaucratic orientation
was largely determined, and heightened, by the nature of Russia's
administrative personnel. In a sense, the officials themselves prevented the formation of a genuine bureaucracy on the Western
model. Not until late in the nineteenth century, and only in the
upper ranks of the hierarchy at that, did there develop anything
like a sense of professional responsibility, technical competence, an
*esprit de corps,* and a set of ethical norms reflecting the social responsibilities of the bureaucracy. Of course, the maintenance of the
autocracy was in itself the primary cause of the situation, for it

---

[5] S. Monas, *The Third Section: Police and Society in Russia under Nicholas I* (Cambridge, Mass.: Harvard University Press, 1961). For rich and re-
vealing illustrations of the realities of Nicholas's ideal see *Memoiren von
Jacob Iwanowitsch de Sanglen 1776-1831* (Stuttgart: 1894); A. V. Niki-
tenko, *Dnevnik,* 3 vols. (Moscow: 1955-56); and, of course, Herzen's *My
Past and Thoughts.*

robbed the officials of genuine responsibility and prevented them from feeling that they could give definitive solution to any matter of consequence, as the final decision depended on the autocrat, or his personal favorites.

It is difficult to speak of Russian officials as if they were a unitary, well-defined, and relatively homogeneous group.[6] To begin with, we can distinguish two separate categories of government servants: The first consisted of the officials in the strict sense, who possessed a definite place and function according to the Table of Ranks and who, in principle at least, could rise in the hierarchy to positions of influence and control. The second category comprised the copyists and clerks and secretaries. These were outside and below the Table of Ranks, poorly paid and badly educated. Scorned by their superiors and by society, they were demoralized and easy prey to drink and graft. They were caught in a dull routine of copying and processing paper which they did not always understand and for whose contents they were neither responsible nor concerned. Russia's tragedy was that, because of the vastness of the Empire and the ubiquity of the administration, a great role devolved on an officialdom that counted too few well-educated and adequately prepared individuals in its ranks. As a result, the lowly clerk wielded much more influence than was warranted by either his position or his personal qualifications. As the routine of processing papers was at the heart of the administrative machinery, the clerk played a vital role, and by standing, so to speak, at the entrance to every level of the administrative and judiciary hierarchy, he was able to forward papers rapidly or hold them up for a long time. He therefore acted as a barrier between the population and the upper rungs of the administrative ladder, and prevented the high officials from learning the true conditions of the people. The failings of this lower stratum of the bureaucracy helped to undermine the government's effectiveness and prevented the regime from reforming itself. The clerk's low level of education, professional competence, and morality precluded the introduction of any pro-

[6] M. Raeff, "The Russian Autocracy and its Officials," *Harvard Slavic Studies*, IV (1957), pp. 77-91; the same, "L'état, le gouvernement et la tradition politique en Russie impériale avant 1861," *Revue d'Histoire Moderne et Contemporaine* (Oct.-Dec., 1962), pp. 296-305.

gressive and sophisticated improvements in administrative practices and norms. Finally, these features of the lower administrative personnel stymied all intentions and attempts at giving greater responsibility and wider scope for independent action to administrative institutions on the local level.

On the upper levels of the administrative apparatus the situation was different, of course, but in some ways no more satisfactory. Throughout most of the imperial period there was little opportunity for obtaining technical training for the tasks of administration. The official who came from the nobility received a very broad and rather superficial general education, with a strong admixture of eighteenth-century rationalist concepts and a somewhat naïve and mechanistic outlook on questions of social and administrative policy. He was little versed either in the history of his own country or in the traditions of its administration or legal system. The situation changed appreciably for the better in the last third of the nineteenth century, but even then a large proportion of the higher officials had only this unsatisfactory educational background. At least until the middle of the nineteenth century (but still to be found in the reign of Nicholas II), many high officials began their career in the military branches of the state service and were educated in military schools. Shifting to the civilian branch because of reverses in their service fortunes, by the direct command of the monarch, or out of personal considerations, they were ill-prepared for their new duties. They were inclined to apply to the problems of administration, social policy, and justice the attitudes, norms, and conceptions of the military. This led to an overemphasis on external good order, strict obedience, and hierarchical subordination, and the tendency to refer all complicated matters to superiors. When the high official, who usually was also a ranking officer, acted as the direct representative of the Emperor, he tended to exercise his authority on a personal basis, disregarding established rules and procedures and disrupting the regular course of business. It became difficult to avoid the pitfalls of arbitrary and dictatorial decisions, even when they were taken in a good cause. Such personal representatives of the Emperor, although less likely to succumb to corruption and bribery (unless they were on a grand scale), were still very much at the mercy of the will of court factions and prey to court intrigues.

Many highly placed officials not of noble origin were the children of clergymen. After successful studies in the ecclesiastical schools they rose through the ranks of the administrative hierarchy, often after a head start as a private secretary or tutor in the household of an influential dignitary. To the same category belonged the individuals (increasingly more numerous toward the end of the nineteenth century) with professional training and experience who entered government service and rose to occupy positions of responsibility and policy-making importance.[7] The education received by these men, whether in ecclesiastical or professional schools, while excellent for the purpose of mastering the techniques of analysis, rhetoric, and written presentation, did not give much understanding of or contact with actual social conditions. Lowly birth, as well as the submissiveness acquired in ecclesiastical schools, could hardly instill a spirit of enterprise, initiative, and independence. Moreover, the habit, acquired in the course of their schooling, of thinking primarily in terms of abstractions, theories, and universal categories tended to blind them to the variety and complexity of Russian society. Lastly, as they owed everything to the system of promotions, the Table of Ranks, the benevolence of their superiors, and—ultimately—the Emperor, they relied on that system and believed that autocracy was the only satisfactory way to govern a country like Russia. Even those who had spent their childhood close to the people and should have been familiar with their miseries and needs were in fact separated from the lower classes by their schooling and careers; they, too, became a barrier rather than a link between the government and the population.

There were, naturally, many individuals who were not typical of the bureaucracy to which they belonged. At some periods—for example, in the early years of the nineteenth century and during the heyday of Alexander II's reforms—exceptional men were numerous and quite influential. Yet, the over-all picture remained by and large characteristic until the disintegration of the regime, and

---

[7] Among high officials of clerical origin were M. M. Speransky and I. I. Martynov in the reign of Alexander I. K. Pobedonostsev, K. Bunge, S. Witte are examples of professionals and technicians who became ministers. Until the last decades of the nineteenth century, most professionals had been educated in ecclesiastical schools.

it contributed to the very conditions of Russian public life which the reform projects discussed in this volume strove to correct.

It should also be kept in mind that in an autocracy the Emperor is always surrounded by courtiers and court factions. A weak sovereign may easily become the prisoner of such factions. By their nature, court factions are interested only in securing immediate personal benefits for their members. The same may be said of the individual favorite, who may exercise great political influence, but still primarily for his own selfish ends. The harm done by court factions and favorites lies not so much in their selfish grabbing, for a rich country may be able to afford some amount of graft if it makes for smoother operation of the government. The greatest threat to a harmonious and beneficent relationship between the ruler and his people stems from the fact that such favorites monopolize access to the ruler's ear. Only the information they are willing to transmit, and in the form they transmit it, can come to the monarch's attention; thus, only one side of a case may ever be known to the ruler. The opportunities for arbitrary, capricious, and unjust decisions are great, and so is the lack of continuity and permanence and the insecurity that such a situation generates. As we shall see, most reform projects in the eighteenth and early nineteenth centuries aimed at eliminating this interference of favorites and factions and substituting for it regularity of procedure; that is, sought to replace the personal element by the bureaucratic.

Implied in our discussion so far has been the existence of what was perhaps the basic problem of Russian political and administrative life throughout the eighteenth and nineteenth centuries: the inadequacy of the channels of communication between the government and the nation. The central offices and policy-making officials in St. Petersburg depended entirely on the written reports of their subordinates. In view of the quality of this personnel, these reports were highly unreliable as well as incomplete. The Emperor's subjects were normally unable to obtain a hearing by relatively high officials, except by accident, through the intervention of well-placed friends, or with the help of bribery. Equally serious was the government's inability to inform the population of its true intentions and of the purpose of its decisions and legislation. Peter the Great had used legislation for civic education, to inform his subjects of his aims, and to impart to the people notions of rational government. His successors did not follow his practice, and in any event it is doubtful that even Peter had been very successful in his efforts. Cut off from direct contact with the country at large, imbued with only vague and general theoretical notions of government, high officials in St. Petersburg rarely conceived that it would be desirable to communicate with the people or allow the people to communicate with them. Many decrees, laws, and statutes were issued in such a way as to remain unknown (if not actually hidden) to the majority of the population concerned, including the educated classes. Even the lower officials were not always adequately informed of the legislation or regulations they might have to enforce.

A second serious problem for the Russian government, largely the product of the features we have just discussed, was the need for better coordination of decisions and policies. In principle, the sovereign was the source of all law and the final instance of appeal for all matters of administration and justice. But he could not possibly coordinate all facets of public life himself. This was especially the case when the ruler was not quite equal to his task, as happened all too frequently. Much legislation was of an *ad hoc* nature to cover specific cases and was not always known even to all the officials who might be concerned. Codification was not achieved until 1835, and even then the former practice of *ad hoc* decrees and rulings kept cluttering the books without being brought into harmony with the provisions of the code.

Perhaps of greater significance than lack of harmony in the laws was the absence of coordination in the administration itself. There was no single institution specifically entrusted with this function. Peter the Great had intended the Senate to play this role, but after his death the Senate's authority declined, and it eventually became primarily a supervisory body and high administrative tribunal. There were brief periods during which the Senate acted as the agent of centralization for the administration (but not as coordinator of legislative policy), as under Elizabeth and to some extent also under Catherine II. Throughout the eighteenth century and in the first years of the reign of Alexander I efforts were made to restore to the Senate this function of coordination (see Documents 2, 3, and 4 in the second part of this volume). But it was believed in high government circles that delegating functions of policy coordination to the Senate could give it an authority and power that might enable it to exercise some measure of control, and in so doing put a limit to the autocratic absolutism of the monarch. Thus, this solution was never accepted. Similar considerations in the nineteenth century prevented the Committee of Ministers from exercising functions of legislative coordination. Attempts were also made to secure greater coherence and consistency of policy by means of special councils that would assist the ruler while being completely under his control. Yet, again and again, universal fear of the rule or influence of an oligarchy prevented such plans from being implemented in full.

In a paradoxical way, perhaps, the lack of adequate coordination of legislation and administration made it possible to preserve the power of autocracy intact into the twentieth century. As the ruler's decision was required in so many matters, he was able to issue *ad hoc* legislation at will. No group of men could challenge the autocracy's supremacy by virtue of their regular administrative functions. Yet at the same time inadequate policy coordination paralyzed the monarch's autocratic power on a day-to-day level. Indeed, his will could easily be betrayed by subordinate officials, who were in a position to act arbitrarily according to their own whim without being called to account, as there was no effective system of coordination and control.[8] While the situation improved immeasurably in the second half of the nineteenth century with respect to social and economic policies, lack of policy coordination continued to have a disastrous effect on the strictly administrative and political aspects of Russia's public life until the outbreak of the revolution.

The rulers of Muscovy had succeeded in preventing the development of social classes into estates, and the population of Russia had been "atomized" quite early in its history. The absolute power of the autocrat had destroyed whatever feeble manifestations of an estate structure had struck roots among the nobility. The reforms and modernization of Peter the Great eliminated the last remnants

---

[8] The best-known and most glaring example of such an abuse of authority was the governorship of I. B. Pestel in Siberia (1805-19).

of a decaying pattern. The elements of regional and class solidarity had never been strong among the peasant population because of the great nobility of its members. The feeble expressions of such solidarities were nipped in the bud by the spread of serfdom and completely destroyed by the poll tax, which turned the peasant into the property of an individual owner who could easily and arbitrarily disrupt at any time his serfs' attachments to a village or region. The clergy had never enjoyed the privileged status of its counterpart in the West. What did bind together members of the same class or group were family relationships (or tribal and clan loyalties, if we follow the terminology popular in Russian historiography in the nineteenth century). But for political purposes, ties and solidarities based on family connections are not so strong as the bonds between members of an estate. In a sense, family loyalties separate or oppose individual families quite as much as they bind together the members of the same family. In Russia individual families (or clans), particularly among the nobility, rose and fell as the Tsar's favor was bestowed or withdrawn from their members, but these families were not able to act in unison to secure rights and privileges of benefit to each and all of them. It would be impossible at this point to go into detail about the reasons for and origins of this situation. Suffice it to note that the two opposed principles of birthright and service achievement helped to keep the nobility divided: nobles who advocated special status on the basis of individual service merits came into conflict with those who claimed status on grounds of birthright. Peter the Great's Table of Ranks gave the conflict a new form, but preserved the nobility's basic lack of cohesion. As rank was strictly personal and not transmissible to others in the family, it could not survive as a basis for estate solidarities and privileges and was even contrary to them. Even the Charter of 1785 did not succeed in transforming the Russian nobility into a genuine estate. The paramount role of rank kept the nobility an open and divided class. Quite naturally, the sovereign was only too happy to preserve a situation that worked to his own advantage. The cities and their burghers were few, economically weak, and very much dependent on the sovereign's favors, and thus could not be the mainstay of a strong third estate as in France.

Consequently, the individual Russian, including the members

of the upper classes, faced the autocrat and the apparatus of the state alone. Naturally, he could not have a strong sense of security, with respect either to his person or to his property and status. Needless to say, the situation was twice as bad for the peasant, who stood in the same isolated and insecure position with respect to his master. Even after 1861 he did not obtain full security, as he remained under the control of his commune as well as of the agents of the government.

Three basic elements, therefore, determined the efforts at government reform which we observe in the eighteenth and nineteenth centuries: (1) the desire to establish regular channels of communication between the government and the population; (2) the need to coordinate and harmonize more effectively the policies of the government; and (3) the wish to invest the relationship between the government and the governed with security of person, property, and status to the latter. The greater attention paid at various times to one or another of these three elements allows us to distinguish several major periods in the efforts at reform over a span of almost two centuries.

One may liken Peter the Great to a man who is trying to erect a house while hurricane winds are blowing overhead. Part of the structure collapses almost immediately under the next gush of wind, and while repairs are made to it, there is no time to complete the other parts or to lay solid foundations. The government edifice Peter left at his death in 1725 resembled a cluster of more or less completed, more or less well-built structures, poorly integrated both among themselves and in relation to the landscape. Peter had rushed to complete as much as he could, breaking up a great deal of the old edifice, and in so doing completely disregarding the needs of individuals. He had driven everyone hard, no matter what the consequences; the pace had been furious, and the nation was exhausted. Not surprisingly, therefore, the first concern of the service noblemen Peter had helped to bring into being by means of the Table of Ranks was to catch their breath, consolidate their gains, and acquire some sense of security and stability.

The first years after the death of Peter were quite confusing; emperors and empresses followed one after another in rapid succession, and their powerful favorites were more short-lived still. The sense of insecurity was at a peak, for every change in the power constellation at court or in government affected deeply the fortunes of many service noblemen. Loss of favor, moreover, meant not only removal from a position of influence but frequently loss of personal liberty and confiscation of property as well. An additional reason for profound insecurity stemmed from the fact that, while the old, traditional order of social relations, especially with regard to the upper classes, had been shattered or even completely destroyed by Peter's reforms, the new rules and relationships had not yet taken hold. In the absence of a feeling of stability, permanence, or coherence, individual members of Russia's nobility felt very much disoriented, socially as well as personally.

The first opportunity to vent these feelings publicly and to suggest ways for dealing with them came in 1730 on the accession of Empress Anne. The documents included in this volume should give an idea of the major concerns and attitudes of the spokesmen of the post-Petrine generation. Yet the crisis was ended with Anne's resumption of absolute and unlimited autocratic power without a satisfactory solution for the basic problems of stability and security. *In the long run,* members of the nobility were given a measure of satisfaction on some of their aspirations, such as greater freedom in disposing of their property, more opportunities for the education of their children, liberalization of the rules of service. But they did not obtain the "right" to security for their person and property. As a matter of fact, Anne's reign was quite tyrannical and arbitrary; the individual privileged service nobleman remained as much the sovereign's *kholop* as his ancestors had been. His property, his life, and his status were entirely at the mercy of the monarch's whims and subject to the tyranny of high officials and favorites.

One of the reasons for this state of affairs was the fact that Russia did not have an up-to-date, comprehensive code of laws. The last code had been drawn up in 1649, and its provisions had to a great extent been rendered obsolete by the profound transformations in Russian government and society wrought by Peter the Great. In the absence of a comprehensive modern code, the conflicts between old and new juridical norms and social values, between the demands of reason and will and those of tradition, could not be settled or reconciled. Peter had recognized the necessity of bringing the elements of historical tradition into harmony with those imported from the West. To this end he had called together the first commission on codification, but it did not do the job, nor did the many that followed it in the eighteenth century or in the first quarter of the nineteenth century (codification was finally carried out by Speransky in 1833). Yet by their very existence, the commissions on codification (some of which were made up of elected or appointed representatives of the upper classes) had at least two effects: they helped to introduce and popularize notions of modern law, in particular natural law; and they were instrumental in making the Russian elite conscious of the fact that their security—both as individuals and as a group—could be safeguarded only by fundamental and stable laws. Codification, therefore, became a symbol of progress and reform, just as much as a constitution or administrative reorganization. At the same time, though, it fostered the belief that all the problems of Russia could be solved by an acceptable code and thus abetted the almost natural propensity of the westernized educated elite for theoretical, "radical," and universal solutions, and their tendency to see basic political problems solely in juridical terms. To put it differently, it fostered the elite's tendency to think in terms of the ends of government rather than of the means.

The technical question of governmental efficiency was of still more immediate concern. The problem of policy coordination took on a very serious aspect after the disappearance of the ruler of genius whose unbounded energy had kept things together and moving in the same direction. The fact that Peter's successors were unusually weak and ill-fitted for their task only compounded the difficulty. In the minds of contemporaries, moreover, the problem of coordination also involved the monarch's lack of communication with his subjects, at least with the nobility. Indeed, not only were noblemen relatively few, but most of their time was spent in government service, so that a proper organization of administrative institutions operating in harmony and unison would enable the voice of the nobility to be heard easily at all levels. Of course, no ruler has ever managed without councilors and advisers. Wise selection of these advisers and stability of membership in the mon-

arch's council could have insured the necessary degree of coordination and supervision in a relatively simple system. The *Boiar Duma*
(and, toward the end of the seventeenth century, its inner council,
the *blizhniaia duma*) had performed this function in Muscovite
Russia relatively well. In organizing the Senate, Peter the Great
hoped to create both the sovereign's deputy for matters of routine
and the coordinating center of the administration. After his death,
however, the function of coordinating policy was taken over by the
Supreme Privy Council. In spite of its bad reputation, the Council
did its job reasonably well. It was staffed with energetic men who
had risen in the service of Peter and who were able to exercise
power effectively. The Council's one major defect, however, was the
fact that most of its members were also the personal favorites of
the sovereign. As long as these were the "fledglings from Peter's
nest," the Council functioned despite the corruption and graft of
its members. But when the membership was enlarged in the reign
of Peter II to include mediocre members from the Dolgorukov
clan, it degenerated. It fell victim of its own ill-fated attempt to
impose "conditions" on Anne. But the various projects drafted in
1730 show an awareness of the need for a coordinating and policy-
making group of advisers.

Even though she rejected the suggestions made in 1730, Anne
had to establish some coordinating center. Her solution was the
Cabinet of Ministers, whose leading spirits, A. Osterman, A. Cherkasskii, and A. Volynskii, were able men who could do an effective
job. Unfortunately, as with everything else in those years, the Ministers were also entirely dependent on the support and good will of
Anne's personal favorites, especially Biron. The Conference of Ministers established in the reign of Elizabeth had basically the same
character as Anne's Cabinet; in addition, it dealt almost exclusively
with matters of foreign policy.

N. Panin's project (Document 2 below) was the most important of the many efforts made at that time to give the sovereign's
council a stable membership, clearly defined functions, and a full
role in coordinating, supervising, and stabilizing policies. Panin
and others clearly saw that such a council or institution would in
fact share in the sovereign's legislative burden, for, in the final analysis, it would have to prepare, present, discuss, and decide on essen-

tial legislation with all the evidence and information at hand. Many who counted solely on the ruler's personal favoritism interpreted the extensive role of such a council as the first step toward the surrender of the monarch's unity of sovereignty and authority. The fear of oligarchy, which had been so influential in bringing to naught D. M. Golitsyn's plans of 1730, derived its strength from the memory of the events of 1610-13 and the period of appanages in medieval Russia, and its impact was so pervasive that every council of some autonomy, permanence, and stability seemed, to the minds of contemporaries, to harbor a threat to the unity of the Russian state.

In a sense, Panin's failure ends the first period of reform efforts. These had been immature and naïve in many ways; they were directed at lightening the noblemen's burdens of service and attaining some degree of security and permanence. Unable, perhaps, to see their demands in a broader framework, the service noblemen contented themselves with the maintenance of autocracy in the hope that the sovereign, on the basis of his personal relationship to his subjects, would give them satisfaction on an individual basis. Overconcern with the preservation of the unity of sovereignty (natural after periods of civil war or upheaval, as in France after the Wars of Religion or in England in the mid-seventeenth century) leads to a defense of absolutism, for complete unity of sovereignty can be secured only by one absolute ruler.[9]

In the course of the eighteenth century, Russian society, especially the upper class, underwent a profound transformation. This became manifest not so much in the structure and basic social character of the class as in the cultural outlook and activities of its members. In brief, Russian noblemen as a group (including newly created nobles and a few professionals) had come of age: they were now individualized and westernized. The nobleman was individualized in the sense that he had broken out of the closed framework of family and clan solidarities; each member was now on his own, and

---

[9] Carl Schmitt, "Soziologie des Souveränitätsbegriffes und politische Theologie," in M. Palyi, ed., *Erinnerungsgabe für Max Weber* (München-Leipzig: 1923), Bk. II, pp. 1-35.

his position in society depended primarily on his personal achievements within the framework of governmental service. At the same time he had adopted Western customs and was beginning to acquire Western modes of thought. With respect to the latter, it is true, progress was rather slow, especially in the provinces, where the vast majority of the petty gentry was still quite uncouth and uncivilized from a Western European point of view. But the leaders, the men who lived in the capitals and served in commanding positions in the army or administration, had become thoroughly westernized. In our context the most important result was that for the elite, westernization meant acquiring a sense of self-resepect, worth, and dignity. When Catherine II finally prohibited the use of derogatory diminutives and humiliating epithets in official petitions to the ruler, she was wiping away an anachronism. The average educated nobleman no longer thought of himself as a slave (*rab*) or servant (*kholop*) of the ruler; he considered himself a loyal subject and, more important still, a "true son of the fatherland." Naturally, he expected to be treated accordingly, to be secure in his person and property, and to be given public recognition for his class's cultural accomplishments. In short, the Russian nobleman had finally become conscious of his "nobility"; he yearned for the public consideration enjoyed by his Western European counterpart; he was convinced that he ought to have special rights and privileges which could guarantee his status and worth as the cultural and moral leader of the nation.

The acts of 1762 (Freedom from State Service), 1775 (Statute on the Provinces), and especially the Charter of 1785 mark the steps which the government took in recognition of the nobility's new position. A reading of the Charter to the Nobility of 1785 would make it appear that the Russian nobility had obtained the status of a privileged corporation, of an estate, whose members were guaranteed security of person and property as well as a dominant role in the government and in the country. The reality, however, was somewhat different. First of all, the security which the nobility believed they had attained was of a very unstable sort. The nobleman in fact remained at the mercy of the autocrat and his officials. Catherine II made this amply clear by repressive measures against members of the masonic lodges, for example, in the last years of her reign, while her son's disregard of the Charter led to a new height in the capricious and arbitrary treatment of members of the service nobility.[10] Thus, at the beginning of the nineteenth century, the upper classes found themselves once again at the mercy of the personal caprices of the Emperor and his favorites.

The deeper cause for the failure of Catherine's legislation with respect to the nobility's corporate rights and privileges lay not so much in the personality of the ruler as in the emergence of an officialdom separated from the nobility and, at times, even opposed to it. Until the middle of the eighteenth century there had been no clear separation between officials and the rank and file of the nobility in service. As long as the nobility's obligation—and only occupation—was to serve the state, its membership coincided with that of officialdom, even though some officials were not noblemen by birth but had merged into the nobility on reaching a specified rank in the Table of Ranks. The situation began to change by the middle of the eighteenth century. The act of 19 February 1762, "freeing" the nobility from compulsory service, should be seen as the state's declaration of independence from the nobility on the one hand, and, on the other, as an attempt by high and wealthy dignitaries to direct the members of the nobility into new activities. Indeed, as far as can be ascertained, the act of 1762 was "hatched" and prepared by men like the Vorontsovs who wished to see in Russia an aristocracy, an estate of privileged individuals whose main source of power, influence, and status in society would derive from their role as owners of land and serfs. The service nobility was to become independent of state service and to be transformed (on the English model) into an economically active and enterprising landowning "gentry" with a dominant role in local self-govern-

---

[10] It is true that Paul I at times made a show of magnanimity and generous understanding; it is possible that he had the welfare of his people at heart (as in his legislation to limit the obligations of the serfs). But he was also most disrespectful of the rights of his subjects. Paul wanted to be benevolent, but he refused to recognize the *rights* of anyone; in other words, the notion of the sanctity and respect of laws was quite alien to him. See also M. V. Klochkov, *Ocherki pravitel'stvennoi deiatel'nosti vremeni Pavla I*, Zapiski istoriko-filologicheskogo fakul'teta imperatorskogo Petrogradskogo universiteta, vol. CXXXII (Petrograd: 1916).

ment.[11] Be that as it may, with the granting of freedom from state service it became possible for noblemen to have other interests and occupations. True, state service remained the principle activity and norm by which membership in the nobility was gauged. But it was no longer life-long, and for many a nobleman, especially after retirement, other activities began to be of greater interest. Such noblemen gradually dissociated themselves from the government and its officials. As their new economic and cultural interests diverged from the principles and policies of the government, the identity between state and nobility that had dominated Russian public life for well-nigh two centuries gradually disintegrated. This did not yet necessarily imply conflict, but it did mean that the traditional relationship between "society"[12] and government would undergo fundamental changes. The problem of communication mentioned earlier thus took on a new aspect and required a solution in terms of the new, emerging relationships between the ruler and the elite of his subjects.

At the same time the intellectual westernization of the Russian elite was beginning to bear fruit. Under the impact of the philanthropic and enlightened ideas of eighteenth-century Western thought, introduced by members of masonic lodges and a few outstanding individuals like Novikov, the conviction grew that government was for the welfare and prosperity of the people and that good government must be based on the rule of law. It reflected, of course, the Enlightenment's belief in the active and positive role of a good code of laws based on just principles. The more progressive and enlightened members of the Russian nobility had absorbed the basic concepts of natural law (in its eighteenth-century enlightened

---

[11] A. N. Filippov, "K voprosu o pervoistochnikakh 'zhalovannoi gramoty dvorianstvu'," *Izvestiia Akademii Nauk SSSR,* 6th series, 1926, vol. XX, Nos. 5-6 and 7-8; A. N. Kulomzin, "Pervyi pristup v tsarstvovanii Ekateriny II k sostavleniiu Vysochaishei gramoty dvorianstvu Rossiiskomu," in N. Kalachov, ed. *Materialy dlia istorii russkogo dvorianstva,* fascicle 2 (St. Petersburg: 1885); G. V. Vernadskii, "Manifest Petra III o vol'nosti dvorianskoi i zakonodatel'naia komissiia 1754-1766 gg," *Istoricheskoe Obozrenie,* XX (1915), pp. 51-59.

[12] The Russian term *obshchestvo,* as used in historical literature, connotes the educated elite, the public opinion of the enlightened and cultured classes of the nation.

and secular form), as well as belief in the role of positive governmental action for the happiness of the nation, and they increasingly
felt that any kind of reform had to redefine the relationships between monarch and subjects of all classes, not excluding even the
serfs.

Such attitudes led to the conclusion that Russia had to become
an *autocracy based on law,* or, in other words, ruled by an autocrat
respectful of the limitations of self-imposed laws. What at first
glance seems to be a paradoxical formulation (which had a prece-
dent in Roman Law) turns out to be less so if we recall that for
eighteenth-century Russians autocracy connoted primarily absolute
sovereignty, that is, the independent and unitary character of the
Russian state. There was no reason, therefore, why autocracy could
not be combined with a *Rechtsstaat*—a state based on the automatic
and beneficent action of stable, permanent, and fundamental laws
designed to secure the nation's welfare.

The real question was how this desirable end—an end on
which both the "government" and "society," with Paul's reign viv-
idly in mind, would readily agree—could best be attained. Two major schools of thought became manifest, each advocating a specific
approach in the quest for security and the rule of law, on the one
hand, and in planning state policy for the solution of Russia's major social, economic, and administrative problems, on the other.

There were, first, those who put security of person and property above everything else in the firm belief that all other problems
of Russia's public life would find their solution once this security
had been achieved. In a sense they implicitly agreed that the best
government was that which governed least, limiting itself to negative functions such as protection of law and order at home and defense against external enemies. In Russia, they argued, autocracy
was essential if these functions were to be performed well, for only
the autocratic sovereign could preserve the unity of the state and
personally insure just treatment under law for all. It should be
kept in mind, of course, that the defender of this approach ac-
counted only for those subjects who might be said to constitute the
*pays légal* of the time, that is, the nobility and those from other
social groups (such as townspeople, merchants, clergy, foreigners)

who were personally free and able to engage in economic and professional activities in their own name.

The aim of this first school of Russian public opinion was to secure fundamental and inalienable rights for the Russian nation; these might vary from one group or class to another, but they would be immutable and absolute. In a sense, the aim was to promote the emergence of genuine estates (in the late medieval, European meaning of the term), or, to put it in somewhat different words, to create social classes, each with its clearly defined juridical character. One of the principal features of the proposals made along these lines was the establishment of some institutional framework to safeguard fundamental rights granted by the Emperor. To this end two different methods were put forward. First was the suggestion that the elective offices established by the Charter of 1785 and the Statute on the Provinces of 1775 serve as the source for some body (or bodies) that would have the right to bring to the attention of the government any abuse of power and violation of basic rights and privileges. In the second place—and on the whole it was the more popular as well as the more realistic approach—were the proposals to invest the Senate with the authority to safeguard basic rights and to supervise the officials with respect to the lawful performance of their duties. Some projects went on to suggest that the membership of the Senate might include some elected or appointed representatives from provincial assemblies of the nobility and municipal assemblies of major towns. The basis for assigning individuals to a particular class was never debated in full, and no consensus emerged. Yet in the last years of the eighteenth century and the first years of the nineteenth, the belief grew that achievement in the economic domain should be given consideration along with birthright and service-acquired status. In any event, the fruits of man's acquisitive activities were to be as secure against administrative arbitrariness and abuse as the person and status of the service nobleman.

The pattern of political reform just outlined has often been branded reactionary or conservative. The first epithet is, of course, grossly inaccurate, for the aim of such reform was different from anything Russia had known before. In terms of Russia's historical tradition and experience, the proposals of those who have often been called the Senatorial party (because of their reliance on a re-organized Senate as the lynchpin of the new order) had no real ante-cedents.[13] But their proposals certainly were conservative, in the Burkean sense: they provided for some change, or more precisely, for the creation of a basis for gradual evolution along novel lines, but not a radical departure from trends that might have been no-ticed by careful observers in the last years of the eighteenth cen-tury. Nor were these proposals uninfluenced by foreign models which had been studied, examined, and debated by prominent rep-resentatives of eighteenth-century Russian public opinion. The most influential model was, of course, England, with whom some leaders of the Senatorial party had close connections. The examples, closer to home, of Prussia, Austria, or Sweden and Poland did not attract much attention at the time.

To introduce genuine estates implied favoring a gradual evo-lution and slow transformation. Observing that the *Ständestaat* is capable of evolving into either enlightened absolutism or parlia-mentary monarchy, Otto Hintze noted that in both cases there is a dispersion of power among well-established and secure legal groups of social classes.[14] Although Europe has experienced only the two alternative developments noted by Hintze, we cannot say, of course, into what other forms the *Ständestaat* might have evolved under different political, social, and economic circumstances. This "open endedness"—its unpredictability and reliance on gradual and un-directed change—made the *Ständestaat* unpopular with eighteenth-century reformers, whether from the camp of the *philosophes* or of the royal bureaucrats. As Roscoe Pound has observed, it was pe-culiarly ill-adapted to a society or cultural climate which had an optimistic faith in human reason and was eager to use its creative will to transform social and political relationships in the light of a

---

[13] It would be possible, though perhaps a little far-fetched, to link the argu-ments and plans of the Senatorial party with the notions of Prince Kurb-skii, the "sworn charter" exacted from Basile Shuiskii, and the "condi-tions" of the Supreme Privy Council in 1730.

[14] O. Hintze, "Typologie der ständischen Verfassungen des Abendlandes," "Weltgeschichtliche Bedingungen der Repräsentativverfassung," *Staat und Verfassung* (Leipzig: 1941).

clearly perceived goal.[15] This explains why the *Ständestaat* broke down in the West in the eighteenth century and also why it failed to strike roots in Russia.

Intent on preserving the role of reason and will, in the tradition of Peter the Great, many wished to reserve exclusively for the government the right and power to shape the country by positive and creative action. They wanted to endow governmental policies with the conscious awareness of specific goals to work for. Security of person and property against arbitrary and tyrannical action of officials had to be guaranteed, of course. But to attain the specific goals (to increase Russia's power and secure the people's welfare) it was essential to coordinate effectively the government's legislative and administrative policies. Hence the idea of streamlining the government's *organization* to provide for both security and coordination. Implied also was the hope that institutional reorganization would result in better communication between the autocrat and his subjects, not through representatives of estates, but through an administrative setup that would make it possible to bring any problem and injury to the attention of regularly established, competent authorities. Clearly, such an organizational reform could be best accomplished, without undermining the autocrat's power, through sovereign command. The ruler himself could only welcome such an approach and such a goal, for they would facilitate the task of government through a better division and distribution of functions.

After the approach proposed by the Senatorial party had been rejected by Alexander I as a danger to the autocracy, those who advocated what might be called the "bureaucratic" approach were invited to submit concrete projects of reform. For about a quarter of a century experiments were made with quite a large number of projects and proposals; some were discussed by the closest advisers of the Emperor, a few received partial application, but none was ever adopted and carried through in its entirety. These projects shared one essential characteristic: they were all concerned with the mechanics of coordinating administrative policies and, to a lesser degree, with setting up a mechanism by which the govern-

---

[15] R. Pound, *Interpretations of Legal History* ("Cambridge Studies in English Legal History," Cambridge: 1930).

ment would be better informed of what was happening in the country.

One of the institutional innovations was the creation of ministries to replace the old colleges that had already begun to disappear. But the problem of adequate coordination was not solved thereby. Indeed, Emperor Alexander I and all his successors were adamant in their refusal to bring together the heads of the ministries into a "cabinet" to develop coordinated policies and offer their collective advice and counsel to the monarch. The Committee of Ministers was merely an occasional meeting of several ministers; it had no policy-making role and only limited administrative authority. Another attempt to coordinate imperial legislation was the establishment of the Council of State, as proposed in Speransky's Plan of 1809. It was to have some of the functions envisaged by Panin for his imperial council, but in addition it was to enjoy an autonomous and rather broad advisory role within the framework of the other institutional reforms proposed by Speransky. But when the Council of State was set up, the remainder of the Plan was "sent to the archives"; torn from its context and its main architect disgraced, the Council of State rapidly sank to the role of a mere editorial board for drafting new legislative acts. As such it survived to the revolution of 1905; no doubt it performed a useful function, but it had no role in directing or coordinating policy.[16]

So far our discussion has been based on the implicit view that the Russian Empire was a unitary, centralized state, administered as if it were made of one piece, with little or no regard to the great variety in its geographic and human makeup and the still greater variety of its regional historical traditions. After the wars against Napoleon some attention was at last paid to the Empire's multinational character. This new interest and concern was probably in large part the result of the incorporation of the Grand Duchy of Finland and the personal union that bound the constitutional Kingdom of Poland and the Russian monarch. In addition, it was becoming obvious, even to conservative officials, that

---

[16] All other projects of the period bore primarily on limited technical aspects of Russia's administration and suggested merely mechanical improvements. They need not, therefore, be taken up here.

the growing complexity of social and economic problems and the resulting need for better coordination between local and central administrative authorities required some reform action. More effective supervision of local institutions was necessary because the quality of the lower clerical personnel had not improved much over the last century: it had not kept pace with the greater needs and sophistication of an ever-growing proportion of the population. If the government wanted to exercise effective leadership in bringing about economic and social progress, it had to direct local institutions into taking account of specific variations in the physical and human environment.

Several proposals were made to take care of this need. Two approaches may be distinguished: The first was to create lieutenancies or governor-generalships by combining several provinces, so that their combined appointed chief, the governor-general, could act as the personal representative of the monarch. The governor-general was not supposed to participate directly in day-to-day administration, but was expected to coordinate and supervise the actions of local authorities, seeing to it that laws and rights were respected and regulations applied in the spirit in which they had been issued by the sovereign and his ministers. The other approach, in a way less bureaucratic, was to give fairly extended rights of self-government to more or less representative bodies within each of the larger subdivisions of the Empire. The most elaborate, as well as the most radical, of such proposals was drafted by N. N. Novosiltsev (Document 7). His major source of inspiration was clearly the constitution of the Republic of Poland before its partition. The obvious fact that his proposal led to the dispersal of the Emperor's authority, if not actual division of his sovereignty, made it quite unacceptable, and no part of it was ever implemented. The experiment of a "federal" solution was not renewed, and all later projects of reform treated the Empire as a single unit with little regard to the special character of its constituent parts. Naturally, such disregard only increased the lack of communication and understanding between the Emperor and the central government, on the one hand, and those of his subjects who differed in language, custom, religion, and culture from the Russians, on the other.

Efforts at mechanical adjustments and improvements of the

administration lasted, in a sense, into the reign of Nicholas I. Only the outbreak of the revolutions of 1848 in the West put a halt to all discussion of reform. None of the secret committees set up by Nicholas I to formulate administrative and social reform helped to bring about better understanding or communication between the nation and the government. Quite the contrary; as they were secret, their discussions remained unknown to the people, and they could not seek the cooperation of influential leaders of public opinion.

Nicholas I was extremely suspicious of Russian educated society and cut it off completely from the government. He also was aware, however, of the government's need for better information on what was going on in the Empire. In the absence of trustworthy officials, efficient institutions, or representative bodies, supervision of the administration and redress of its wrongdoings had to be the task of the ruler himself. To this end he created the Third Section of His Own Chancellery and the Corps of Gendarmes. Their failure and perversion of their mission into a kind of secret and ubiquitous political police must have made it obvious to all that even in Russia genuinely effective personal and patriarchal king-ship was not possible any more.[17]

The reforms of Alexander II, above all the emancipation of the serfs, helped to usher in extensive changes in Russian society. These changes were bound, of course, to affect the country's public institutions and the pattern of its administration; the resulting transformation might be described as an acceleration of the process of modernization or of the establishment of a modern industrial society in Russia. In the context of our discussion, we might say more specifically that the reforms of Alexander II—in particular

---

[17] In one respect, however, the "technological" approach to administrative reform yielded positive results. The compilation of the Code in 1833, un-der the chairmanship of Speransky, made it possible at last for the rule of law to prevail in ordinary civil affairs, although it was not until the reforms of the 1860's that an independent and honest judiciary came into being. For a sympathetic summary of the administration of Nicholas I, see N. V. Riasanovsky, *Nicholas I and Official Nationality in Russia, 1825-1855* (University of California Press: 1959), and for a perceptive sketch of Nicholas I as man and ruler (too favorable to its subject, perhaps), see C. de Grunwald, *La vie de Nicolas I$^{er}$* (Paris: 1946).

the emancipation, the *zemstvo* organization, and the reorganization of the judiciary—led to an expansion of the role of administration. The role of governmental institutions was expanded because of the ever-increasing complexity of Russian life, particularly of economic life, in which the government took a lively interest by participating in the development of industry and transportation. Industrialization and its accompanying social and economic problems required the government's active involvement in matters related to public health, social legislation, urban control, and the like. Furthermore, the government had to meet new responsibilities and face greater challenges in connection with the establishment of the *zemstvo* institutions and the reformed judiciary. The greater professionalization of life led to deeper governmental involvement in controlling and supervising education, cultural activities, and the press. If, as had been its wont since Peter the Great, the Russian state wished to preserve its leadership and keep under strict control most facets of public life, it had to expand its functions, which meant increasing the number of officials and providing them with greater technical competence.

The institutional structure inherited from the past (its basic organization was not to change appreciably in the half century preceding the revolution of 1905) had difficulties in adapting and keeping pace with the emerging new social and economic realities. The unwieldy machine creaked and puffed, yet somehow it did hold together and managed to perform. This was not so much the result of its flexibility as of the emergence of many new institutions capable of performing public functions without actually being part of the government. As a result, a greater number of professionally trained people became available to staff both private and public institutions; new blood could be pumped into the bureaucracy. The officials whose characterization was discussed earlier were gradually giving way to a regular, genuine bureaucracy, a body of men trained for their tasks, acting according to set rules, possessing a degree of professionalism and continuity as a body. These new officials had a genuine sense of civic responsibility (within the limits set by the existing political regime, of course); they were not altogether blind to nor uncritical of the evils of the political system, and they desired to improve it.

Unfortunately, this change in the character of Russia's administrative personnel was taking place only on the higher-middle level of the hierarchy. In other words, the clerks remained much the same as their predecessors of the eighteenth and early nineteenth centuries: ill-prepared, incompetent, demoralized, as well as open to graft and corruption; the compensatory mechanism of their petty tyranny still weighed most heavily on the lower classes of the population. Nor was there any change at the very top of the pyramid. In the absence of a responsible and coherent ministry and effective institutions of administrative coordination and supervision, the absolute ruler depended on his courtiers, personal friends, and advisers picked up by chance. The most trusted top advisers of the last three Emperors were a very mixed group. Some were efficient and remarkable professionals or experts (for example, Pobedonostsev, Bunge, Witte). Some others had had brilliant careers in the military or civil administration (Miliutin, Valuev, Stolypin). Yet at the same time great influence—at times the dominant one—was exercised by courtiers and members of the imperial family. In some cases these personal favorites worked well (Rostovtsev, Lanskoi, Grand Duke Constantine), but in many more they worked very badly indeed. Personal favorites, as in the eighteenth century, still could play a major role, as witness the genesis of the Russo-Japanese War or, on the eve of the imperial regime's final collapse, the incredible influence of Rasputin. The Emperor worked with each dignitary separately, and in addition he listened to the advice of courtiers and personal aides and favorites. Little wonder that there was no stability, coherence, and continuity in policy decisions. After conferring with the Emperor and securing his assent to a proposal, even the most influential and important minister or councilor could not be sure that he would obtain permission to implement his project. Every minister tried to be the last to see the Emperor to prevent unfavorable advice from reaching the Emperor before signature of his reports. The ruler was not unaware of the situation, but he permitted it, for it allowed him to retain control of the government, something the weaker monarchs were always worried about.

Thus, petty tyranny, corruption, and arbitrariness reigned at the bottom level of the administration, oppressing and exploiting the small people. On the middle level, highly competent and more responsible officials displayed a genuine desire to respond adequately to the country's needs and problems; they tried their best to bring legality and order into the administration. On the very top, auto-cratic absolutism continued its arbitrary and capricious rule. The existence of these three levels explains the long survival of the regime as well as its basic weakness and eventual total collapse. The revolution of 1905 postponed the ultimate reckoning by giving greater scope and strength to the middle-level officials and by starting the improvement of the lower. But even it proved in-capable of genuinely transforming the character of the top level of Russia's government. The consequence was 1917.

The reforms of the 1860's and 1870's had their greatest impact on institutions and activities not directly dependent on the govern-ment. In spite of many onerous restrictions, the peasant was now free to pursue his economic self-interest. In addition, peasant in-stitutions, especially the commune, had more numerous and signif-icant functions than ever before. After the emancipation we witness the reform of local government and the establishment of the *zemstvos*. As is well known, the *zemstvos* took on important func-tions in the realms of education, welfare, public health, and eco-nomic and social protection. In addition they provided men and women with an opportunity of doing socially useful and responsible work without becoming part of the official bureaucracy. The same might be said of the judiciary; although judges and procurators were still government officials, the new system gave rise to an in-fluential and well-trained class of lawyers.

Equally significant was the fact that new social groups and classes—entrepreneurs, merchants, traders, financiers, workers, en-gineers, managers, accountants—were establishing private organiza-tions and associations to promote their particular interests and concerns. They were thereby laying the groundwork for a plural-istic society.[18] This development found further expression in the growing role of the press and those organizations which provided

---

[18] Useful information may be found on these associations in J. Walkin, *The Rise of Democracy in Pre-Revolutionary Russia (Political and Social Insti-tutions under the Last Three Czars)* (New York: Frederick A. Praeger, 1962).

education and a place for public exchanges of ideas—for example, schools, universities, and learned societies. These new institutions naturally demanded that their lawful activities be free and secure from arbitrary administrative interference; they wanted the right to expand and maximize their contribution to the welfare, prosperity, and cultural growth of the Russian people.

A new dilemma thus made its appearance in Russian public life, new at least in its scope and intensity: government guidance and control or free initiative of private associations and professional groupings. While the old tradition of state leadership and control maintained itself on the very top of Russia's governmental structure, Russian society had been striking out more and more on its own and at a much more rapid pace than the government was willing to admit. Paradoxically, perhaps, as the work of Peter the Great came to fruition, it destroyed that very basis of a community of interests between government and society that had been its aim. Indeed, Peter the Great had viewed the state's role of leadership as a *means* for bringing out the economic and spiritual potential inherent in the nation and for raising Russia to the level of Western Europe. Once this was accomplished, Peter believed, the interests of the state and of the individual members of society would merge to further the greatness and glory of Russia. By the second half of the nineteenth century the government had done its job relatively well, and it had helped to bring into being new forces and sources of power for the Russian nation. But these forces then began to demand greater freedom of action and more scope for their growth, while the government found it impossible to abandon its leadership and control of society. The effort made in the reign of Alexander I to lay the foundation for a new relationship by giving private endeavor a larger role and greater freedom was stifled by the bureaucratic approach to institutional reform and the decision to preserve autocracy intact.

The more enlightened members of the government realized that without the participation and help of "public opinion" (as represented by leading circles of Russia's educated classes) it would be impossible to carry out peacefully the great transformation of Russian society implicit in the emancipation of the serfs. Thus, work on the emancipation itself was carried on with the help and advice of selected individuals or groups of the enlightened elite. In the years immediately following, the same approach was taken in working out the *zemstvo* legislation and judicial reform. Russia's elite thus came to hope that it would continue to be asked to collaborate with the administration; such a collaboration had been made easy by the creation of an appropriate institutional framework through the *zemstvos*, universities, technical commissions, and professional associations. But, as is well known, the government betrayed this hope and turned a deaf ear to the pleas of public opinion. In the eyes of the administration the growth of the revolutionary movement and its increasing violence justified repressive policies and efforts at maintaining strict controls over most aspects of public life. Thus, the expected collaboration between government and public opinion did not materialize, and, worse still, the government lost the confidence and support of even the moderates, who began to protect and finance revolutionary agitation. Clearly, the break of communication between society and the state was at its most serious. An unfortunate byproduct of this break was the government's increasing inability to secure adequate information on what was really going on in the country. Officials believed that the representatives of public opinion had no business suggesting anything pertaining to matters of administration and treated critical information and complaints alike as expressions of subversive sentiment. The catastrophic effect of the famine of 1892 was in large part due to this breakdown in communication.

The more intelligent and enlightened officials realized the danger this situation presented to the country's political and social structure, and they bent their efforts at breaching the gap. Their proposals of reform aimed at establishing the means to keep open regular and good communication between society and government. The difficulty was to bring about this communication without permitting the representatives of public opinion to participate in the actual process of legislation or government. One way of circumscribing the role of advisory representatives of society was to limit strictly the circle of potential participants. In other words, the *pays légal* (those permitted to elect and be elected) was to be kept very small by all kinds of restrictions, mainly property qualifications. It was not only a matter of property, however, but also of class status; preference was given to the landed nobility in the belief that they would be the most loyal and moderate. One glaring weakness of these projects was the scant respect paid to the multinational character of the Russian Empire. Border regions and most non-Russian minorities were in fact given inferior status and not permitted to participate on an equal basis with the Great Russian population. Such a short-sighted policy was fraught with great dangers for the future, in view of the ever-growing strength of national consciousness and the economic and cultural development of most nationalities within the Russian Empire.

In the final analysis, the imperial regime failed to reform itself from within. Unwilling to abandon the traditions and attitudes developed in the course of the eighteenth century, unable to adjust rapidly enough to the economic, cultural, and social transformation of Russian society, distrusting the free initiative and participation in public affairs of its subjects, the regime could not cope with the growing complexities of the situation it had helped to create. Poorly served by its officials, it lacked the necessary flexibility and courage; incapable of bending, the regime cracked and eventually disintegrated. Yet, not everything is to be blamed on the nature of the imperial government; other factors in Russian society contributed to the final crackup and collapse. In our context the most important of these factors was a failure to develop centers of authority and power outside the framework of government; that is, the absence of strong corporations or estates endowed with privileges, rights, and autonomy of action within their domain.

Russia never became a *Ständestaat,* and the imperial government prevented the creation of a dynamic and flexible *Rechtsstaat.* In spite of all efforts and improvements, the imperial regime could not withstand the stress of modernization and contact with the West. But the very reasons that made it vulnerable also explain why it survived so long: there was no readily available alternative, at least not until a pluralistic society had begun to emerge in the second half of the nineteenth century.

For the two centuries of its existence Imperial Russia struggled to find a flexible and practical solution to the three major problems which it had inherited from its Muscovite past and the reforms of Peter the Great: staffing of the administration, securing communication with the people, bringing about coordination and continuity of basic policy decisions. The solution, however, was sought within the framework of the autocracy and on the basis of the preservation of the paramount role of government. Under conditions of constant expansion, modernization, and westernization, Russia failed to develop the social and political *corps intermédiaires* (Montesquieu) which make possible a rule of law, whether in an absolute or parliamentary monarchy. There was no lack of individuals aware of the basic inadequacies of the Russian body politic. Yet they were unsuccessful in their search for a solution, either because they lacked the insight necessary to break out of the limited outlook that history had imposed on Russia, or because they could not overcome the resistance of the Establishment. But their efforts and failure are worthy of study because they help us to see more clearly and understand better the basic elements in Imperial Russia's social and political structure. They help to explain the final collapse of the system, and at the same time they contribute to our understanding of some basic traits of modern Soviet political and social thought.

# I

# The Succession Crisis
# of 1730

---◦◦◦◆◦◦◦---

### Introduction

By the decree of 5 February 1722 (PSZ, No. 3893), Peter the Great abolished the customary law of succession and provided that every ruling monarch was to appoint his own successor. But neither Peter the Great himself nor his immediate successors ever had a chance of exercising their new right. As a result, the death of each ruler provoked a succession crisis which was settled by the intervention of outside forces and pressures—court favorites, regiments of the Guards, intrigues of foreign diplomats.

When the adolescent Peter II died suddenly on January 19, 1730, having failed to appoint a successor, the contest for the vacant throne was opened again. At the instigation of the capable Prince Dmitrii Mikhailovich Golitsyn, the members of the Supreme Privy Council (which had held most of the powers of government ever since the disgrace and exile of Prince A. D. Menshikov in 1727) offered the crown to the niece of Peter the Great, Duchess Anne of Courland (Anna Ioannovna). Prince Golitsyn, however, felt that this was also an opportunity for restricting the autocratic power of the

Russian monarch and imposed "conditions" *(konditsii)* on the newly chosen Empress.[1] As we shall see, the "conditions" limited the power of the ruler by forcing her to share most of her vital prerogatives with the Supreme Privy Council. In spite of the efforts of Golitsyn and his colleagues to keep their action secret until Anne had arrived in Moscow from her residence (Mitau in Courland), the news leaked out, perhaps not quite accidentally, and spread among the large number of noblemen who had congregated in Moscow for the coronation of Peter II and who had not disbanded after his death.

Forced by the growing agitation and discontent of the nobility and fed by rumors, as well as by the intrigues of some dignitaries— for example, Iaguzhinskii and Osterman—who wanted to destroy the influential Golitsyn and Dolgorukii clans, the Supreme Privy Council invited the noblemen to submit their views and proposals for reforming the government. A series of projects were drafted and submitted for the signature of members of the nobility. There are twelve such projects known to us, identified either by the name of the first signatory or the number of signatures appended to it. Most of these projects show hasty composition and confused thinking;

---

[1] It has been thought—on the fragmentary evidence of reports by foreign diplomats—that Prince Golitsyn conceived of the "conditions" as the first step to the introduction of a genuine constitutional system in Russia. The constitution would have been modeled on the Swedish pattern, giving the major role to the upper rungs of the nobility, while also safeguarding the basic interests of the rank-and-file noblemen and townspeople and improving the lot of the peasantry. But the very existence of such a far-reaching scheme is to be doubted, as W. Recke argued in his frequently neglected study, "Die Verfassungspläne der russischen Oligarchen im Jahr 1730 und die Thronbesteigung der Kaiserin Anna Ivanovna," *Zeitschrift für Geschichte Osteuropas,* II (1911), pp. 11-64, 161-203. Recke's arguments convinced such an outstanding scholar of the eighteenth century as A. Kizevetter ("Dvorianskie politicheskie proekty," *Nauchnye Trudy Russkogo Narodnogo Universiteta v Prage,* II (1929), pp. 77-88), and we follow his interpretation in the present anthology by omitting the alleged constitutional project of Golitsyn. On the basis of a careful review of hitherto neglected or unknown archival materials, the Soviet scholar G. A. Protasov reaches a similar conclusion. G. A. Protasov, *Konditsii i proekty 1730g* (Avtoreferat dissertatsii na soiskanie stepeni kandidata istoricheskikh nauk), Moskovskii oblastnoi pedagogicheskii institut, 1955, and " 'Konditsii' 1730g. i ikh prodolzhenie," *Uchenye Zapiski, Tambovskii pedagogicheskii institut,* XV (1957), pp. 215-31.

they deal mainly with specific concrete demands for relief of hardships created by the patterns of service, inheritance, and justice stemming from Peter the Great's reforms. The main object of attack, however, was the role played by the members of the Supreme Privy Council. It was feared that Russia would fall prey to a narrow oligarchy, that the unity of its sovereignty would be undermined, and that the country would gradually decline to the condition of Poland. Naturally, the general officers, as well as the rank-and-file noblemen, were not so much concerned with Russia's hypothetical future development as worried about the excessive advantages which would accrue to the Supreme Privy Council.

Remembering the rule of court cliques in the seventeenth century and recalling the times when Russian sovereignty had been splintered among several princely families, the rank-and-file noblemen came out against the "conditions." Anne was informed of their sentiments, which were confirmed by the petition Prince Cherkasskii submitted to her. Upon arriving in Moscow she contrived to confront the Supreme Privy Council with the mass of the nobility and have her acceptance of the "conditions" shouted down. She then "deigned to tear up the 'conditions'," and, following suit to the petition submitted by Prince Trubetskoi, she assumed complete autocratic power. She did not fail to make full use of her unlimited prerogatives, and the ten years of her reign may be considered among the most tyrannical and arbitrary of the eighteenth century.

This summary of events should provide the background for the projects reproduced below. We have three distinct orientations: the Supreme Privy Council, whose aims are expressed in the "conditions"; the ideas of the group of general officers, represented by Matiushkin's project and to some extent by Grekov's paper; and the opinions of the rank-and-file noblemen, illustrated by the "outline" and the petitions of Cherkasskii and Trubetskoi. In the final analysis, as shown by the sequence of these projects, the majority of the nobility preferred the re-establishment of full autocratic rule to any kind of "constitutional" or limiting settlement. The old Muscovite traditions, as well as the new pattern of service introduced by Peter the Great, made the nobility completely dependent on the autocracy whose creation they were, so that nothing was expected outside the good graces of the autocratic monarch. The noblemen's political horizon did not extend beyond an expression of hope that the worst abuses and hardships would be alleviated in time (which they were, over a span of three generations). Noteworthy, too, is the absence of any theoretical notions. The only person who had some understanding of the theoretical issues involved and still remained representative of the rank-and-file nobility was V. N. Tatishchev, but even he used his readings and knowledge of Western political theory to advocate the re-establishment of autocracy.[2]

*Conditions Imposed on Empress Anne by the*
*Members of the Supreme Privy Council*
From *Votsarenie imperatritsy Anny Ioannovny*
by D. A. Korsakov (Kazan': 1880). "First Draft," pp. 8-9;
"Final Draft," pp. 17-18.

**First Draft**

Hereby, we firmly promise that my primary concern will be not only the preservation but also, as much as possible, the dissemination of our Greek Orthodox faith. Inasmuch as the integrity and welfare of any state is the result of good counsel, we also promise to retain always the presently existing Supreme Privy Council of eight members, and without the Council's consent [we promise]:

1. Not to start war with anyone;
2. Not to conclude peace;

---

[2] Tatishchev used the arguments from natural law, and more particularly the notion of social contract, to justify, as Hobbes had done, the necessity of undivided sovereignty vested in an absolute, autocratic monarch; cf. his "Proizvol'noe i soglasnoe rassuzhdenie i mnenie sobravshegosia shliakhetstva russkogo o pravlenii gosudarstvennom," 4 February 1730 in *Utro*, 1859, pp. 369-78. In so doing, he was following in the footsteps of Feofan Prokopovich, who had made similar use of Western concepts to justify Peter the Great's decision to change the customs of succession and who, by the same token, had provided theoretical justifications for the autocratic power of the Russian monarch; cf. his treatise *Pravda voli monarshei* (St. Petersburg: 1726).

3. Not to burden our loyal subjects with new taxes;
4. Not to promote to high ranks in either the civil or military services above the grade of colonel and not to appoint anyone to important offices;
5. Not to deprive [members of] the nobility of their life, honor, and property without trial;
6. Not to grant estates and villages;
7. Not to spend state revenue, and to keep all our loyal subjects in our good graces irrevocably.

### Final Draft

Whereas by will of God Almighty and the common wish of all the Russian people we have ascended the imperial throne of All Russia upon the demise of the most glorious and sovereign Lord, Peter II, Emperor and Autocrat of All Russia, our beloved sovereign and nephew, and [whereas] in accordance with God's law [I] intend and wish to rule in such manner as to glorify first God's name and to serve the welfare of our whole state and of all our loyal subjects;

Wherefore, we promise firmly that my main concern and effort will be not only to maintain but also to disseminate as much as possible our Greek Orthodox faith; and upon accepting the Russian crown [I promise] not to enter into bonds of marriage for the duration of my life and not to appoint any heir.[3] And as the integrity and welfare of any state consists in good counsel, we promise to maintain the existing Supreme Privy Council of eight members, and without this Supreme Privy Council's consent:

1. Not to start war with anyone;
2. Not to conclude peace;
3. Not to burden our loyal subjects with new taxes;
4. Not to promote to high ranks (in the civil as well as the military services) above those of colonel, and not to appoint to high office, and to have the Guard and other regiments under the authority of the Supreme Privy Council;

---

[3] This refers to the act of Peter the Great of 5 February 1722 (PSZ, No. 3893), making succession to the throne dependent on appointment by the sovereign.

5. Not to deprive [members of] the nobility of life, property, and honor without trial;

6. Not to grant estates and villages;

7. . . . Not to promote either Russians or foreigners to court offices;

8. Not to spend state revenue;

And to keep all loyal subjects in our good graces irrevocably. And if I do not fulfill or keep any of these promises, I shall be deprived of the Russian crown.

*Project of the Generals (Project of Matiushkin)*[4]
From Korsakov, *op. cit.*, Appendix, pp. 9-11.

1. In our opinion, the present membership of the Supreme Privy Council should be increased by several persons, so that there be a total of twelve or thirteen members. And as the general officers [*generalitet*] and nobility should be called together for important matters concerning the administration or the general weal of the state, as seen in article 6 below, there would be not a small but an oversized assembly. For the conduct of daily routine affairs the above-mentioned number of members is sufficient.

2. For filling vacancies in the Supreme Privy Council, at the present time and in the future, the general officers in the civil and military services and the nobility will elect three candidates for each vacancy and submit them to the Supreme Privy Council, who will then select the most suitable, either by vote or by lot, at their discretion.

3. Alternatively, the Supreme Privy Council may select three candidates, one of whom is then appointed by the general officers from the military, the higher officials, and the nobility. No less than seventy persons have to be present at such an election, and no more than two from one family. Those who select the candidates (that

---

[4] Mikhail Afanas'evich Matiushkin (1676-1737): military and political figure; helped to draft the Table of Ranks act; head of the Chancery for Criminal Affairs.

is, members of the Supreme Privy Council) may not participate in the vote and will be replaced by other persons so that the electoral assembly have a full membership.

4. In our opinion the Senate should have eleven members. The selection of members of the Senate, of presidents of the Colleges, and of governors is left to the Supreme Privy Council, or it may be done by society [that is, the nobility] by ballot. The reason for increasing the number of senators is that some of them will be ordered into the provinces to supervise the governors and *voevodas* [army commanders].

5. There should be no more than one candidate from each family.

6. Everything that will be needed in the future to complete the statutes concerning the state administration *or the common weal* must be confirmed by the common counsel and wish of the Supreme Privy Council, the general officers, and the nobility. [Variant reading: Supreme Privy Council, Senate, general officers, and nobility.]

7. The best system for service promotions of members of the nobility and of the military personnel should be devised and terms set for the service's duration. No one from the nobility should be made [to serve] forcibly as sailor or artisan.[5]

8. To the extent that it is feasible, give satisfaction to the complaints of the nobility, the clergy, the merchants, and of all others, according to their respective status, as this is the foundation and preservation of stable government; as to the peasants, upon adequate investigation, give them some tax relief.

9. Discuss the [rules of] promotion of officers and soldiers and the regular payment of their salaries, setting definite terms for this purpose.

10. Draw up rules for inheritance of real estate and the succession of extinct families for future guidance.

11. As to the capital, for the sake of the common good, we wish it to be in Moscow.

---

[5] Peter's regulations for service required that everyone, including members of the nobility, start service at the bottom of the hierarchy, that is, as ordinary soldiers, seamen, or craftsmen.

12. We humbly request the Supreme Privy Council, if it is agreeable to it, to solicit Her Majesty's assent to all the aforementioned.

(FIFTEEN SIGNATURES)

*First Project of the Nobility (Project of Grekov)*
From *Pamiatniki novoi russkoi istorii—Sbornik istoricheskikh statei i materialov* by V. Kashpirev
(St. Petersburg: 1871), Vol. I, Part 2, pp. 4-5.

On this 7th day of February, in the Supreme Privy Council, at the meeting of the general officers from the military and civil services, the "articles" subscribed to by Her Imperial Majesty, the sovereign Empress, having been read, the [following] was stated in the name of the Supreme Privy Council: whoever can devise something for the greater good of the state and of society, and not for his own personal interest, and who, fearing God's judgment, can give advice in all conscience, let him make himself known. And in accordance with this announcement we submit what we have been able to devise in good conscience for the better benefit of the state and of society, as follows:

(1) To begin with, set up a High Government [authority] of twenty-one persons. (2) And in order not to burden this Government with too many affairs, set up a Senate of eleven [variant: one hundred] members to take care of the other [current] business. (3) The general officers and nobility are to select and vote on candidates to the High Government, the Senate, the governorships, and to the presidencies of the Colleges. And there should be no more than one candidate from any one family, and no more than two persons from one family participating in the election; and the quorum for voting should be no less than one hundred persons, and no members of the candidates' families may participate in the vote. (4) Except for the present members of the Supreme Privy Council, in the future there should be no more than two persons from one family in the High Government and Senate counted together. (5) Important affairs of state and necessary additions to the statutes

pertaining to the government of the state should be drafted and approved by common consultation between the High Government, Senate, general officers, and the nobility. (6) Devise the best system of service for the nobility, so that no one is compelled to serve more than twenty years against his will, and in order not to oblige any noble to serve as sailor or artisan against his will; and, after investigation, render a decision in the case of those nobles who are sailors or artisans at the present time. (7) Give the clergy and the merchants relief from the burden of quartering troops, and give tax relief to the peasantry, as will be estimated proper. (8) Devise an orderly system of promotions and pay for officers and soldiers, so that they will be made at appointed time. (9) Make an examination of retirement and inheritance [rules], and of what is to be done about them in the future. (10) Consider and award compensations and cost of upkeep for those officers and soldiers who are retired for old age and wounds and who do not have their own sources of income.

(SIGNED BY 330 PERSONS)

*"Outline" Submitted to the Rank-and-File Nobility*
From Kashpirev, *op. cit.*, pp. 7-8.

At the present, the following is drafted by the nobility:

1. The Senate should have thirty members. Her Majesty is to preside and have three votes; and there should be no Supreme Privy Council.

2. For [the performance of the] small business, delegate ten members [of the Senate, presumably] every year; but all members are to consult together on matters of state.

3. Members to the Senate should be elected, but there should be no more than two persons from a single family.

4. The army should be under the Military Colleges, while the Guard is to be under the Senate.

5. The nobility is to fill by vote the vacancies occurring in the Senate, the presidencies of the Colleges, and the governorships, and the Senate should not interfere in the elections.

6. Court officials are to be elected anew.

7. In the future, the Diet *(seim)* should devise, and the nobility confirm, whatever is necessary for the reform and welfare of the state.

8. Noblemen should not be appointed to the military ranks of private and artisan, but special companies should be established for them, and for those in the navy, units of marine Guards.

9. The seniority rule in matters of inheritance should be abrogated and complete freedom given to the parents; and, if there are no parents left, the inheritance is to be divided in equal shares.

*Petition of Cherkasskii*[6]
From Korsakov, *op. cit.*, pp. 271-72.

Most glorious and most gracious Sovereign Empress! Although You have been elevated to the throne of the Russian Empire by the will of the Almighty and the unanimous consent of all the people, in testimony of Your high favor to the whole State, Your Imperial Majesty has deigned to sign the articles presented by the Supreme Privy Council, and we thank You most humbly for this gracious intent. Not only we, but also our descendants will have cause to render thanks and display through their words and feelings their sincere respect for Your name in all eternity. However, most Gracious Lady, some of these articles raise such doubts that the majority of the people is in fear of future disturbances, which can benefit only the enemies of our Fatherland; and although, after sober deliberation, we have written down our opinions and presented them to the Supreme Privy Council with all due respect and in all humility, requesting that there be devised a safe system of government for the peace and welfare of the state in accordance with the opinion of the majority, yet, most Gracious Lady, they still have not decided on it, and the written opinions of many have not even been accepted. But they have announced that no decision can be reached without Your Imperial Majesty's will.

---

[6] Prince Aleksei Mikhailovich Cherkasskii (1680-1742): High Chancellor, cabinet minister, and senator.

However, knowing Your Imperial Majesty's natural charity and desire to show favor to the whole Empire, we most humbly and submissively request Your Majesty that You graciously permit to assemble all general officers, officers, and noblemen, one or two from every family, to examine the opinions submitted by us and others, to investigate all circumstances, and, on the basis of the majority's opinion, to devise a form of government for the state and to submit it for Your Majesty's approval.

As to us, we most humbly and dutifully hope, wish [?], and vow our loyalty and the pursuit of Your Majesty's personal interest, and [promise] to honor You as the Mother of the Fatherland, and to glorify You for all centuries to come. Although not many have signed this petition, for it is dangerous to meet and collect signatures, it is approved by the majority, as witnessed by the opinions signed by many but which, as indicated earlier, have not yet been accepted.

*Petition of Prince Trubetskoi*[7]
From Korsakov, *op. cit.*, pp. 275-76.

Most illustrious and most sovereign High Lady, Empress Anna Ioannovna, Autocrat of All Russia!

When Your Imperial Majesty graciously deigned this day to put Your own hand to our humble petition for the better security and welfare of our Fatherland, we had to acknowledge that we were unworthy of expressing gratitude for such an outstanding favor from Your Imperial Majesty. However, the zeal of loyal subjects, which our duty commands, compels us to show ourselves grateful to the extent of our ability; as a sign of our gratitude, therefore, we most humbly submit our request that You graciously resume such *Autocratic* power as Your glorious and praiseworthy ancestors possessed and abrogate the article sent to Your Imperial Majesty by the Supreme Privy Council and signed by You.

We, Your most loyal subjects, only beg Your Imperial Majesty

---

[7] Ivan Iur'evich Trubetskoi (died 1750): General Field Marshal.

that in place of the Supreme Privy Council and the High Senate, You deign to establish a single Governing Senate, as it was under Your Imperial Majesty's uncle, Peter the First of glorious memory; and it would be adequately staffed with a membership of twenty-one persons; and that it also be ordered that the nobility [*szlachta*] elect by ballot to the present membership and fill future vacancies to the above-named Governing Senate, governorships, and presidencies [of the Colleges], as it had been established under Your Imperial Majesty's uncle, Peter I.

And withal, as Your most loyal subjects, we request that a form of administration be now instituted under Your signature for future times. In addition, we, Your most obedient slaves, hope that we will be provided with wise administration, justice, and a lightening of taxation in accordance with Your Imperial Majesty's natural good-heartedness, and that we shall enjoy a quiet and peaceful existence in prosperity and abundance.

Your Imperial Majesty's most humble slaves

(166 SIGNATURES FOLLOW)

# II

# The Memorandum of Count Nikita Panin
## 28 December 1762

## Introduction

The overthrow of Peter III and the accession of Catherine II in June, 1762, had been engineered partly to put a stop to the seemingly arbitrary capriciousness of the Emperor's policy. Catherine desired to remedy the lack of consistency and coherence of government policy which had been endemic ever since the strong hand of Peter the Great had sunk into the grave with the founder of the modern Russian state. One of her earliest supporters and by far the best political head among them, Count Nikita Ivanovich Panin (1718-83) believed that the solution lay in bringing order and coherence to the process by which the monarch reached basic policy decisions.

Panin, whose brilliant diplomatic career had given him good knowledge of the working of the governments of Sweden, Denmark, and England, was convinced that no absolute monarch could rule by himself alone, as he was always in danger of falling victim to the intrigues, deceptions, and selfish goals of his favorites and courtiers.

In the absence of a constitution, which Panin did not envisage for Russia at the time, an imperial council of well-chosen dignitaries should provide the necessary orderliness, coherence, and *esprit de suite* to government. To insure the implementation of legislation devised with the council's help, the Senate should serve as central executive body and be organized along functional lines.

At first approved by Catherine II, Panin's proposals came to naught, however, because she was persuaded by her other advisers that the proposed imperial council would become an instrument for limiting her authority. The fear was even expressed that Panin's scheme was but a new version of Prince D. M. Golitsyn's plan of 1730 to establish the rule of an aristocratic oligarchy.

After this failure, Panin ceased to play a leading part in determining Catherine's domestic policies, although he remained her principal adviser on foreign affairs. As tutor of Grand Duke Paul, however, Panin hoped to influence the future ruler of Russia. But he did not live to see Paul's accession. Toward the end of his life, Panin also became convinced that a mere structural reorganization of governmental institutions along the lines he had suggested in 1762 was not adequate. What Russia really needed were fundamental and permanent laws to safeguard persons and property against the caprices of the monarch and the irresponsible arbitrariness of officials. This was the essence of a manifesto for the accession of Paul which Panin drafted, but again it was not used.[1] Its basic notions, however, were incorporated into the political ideas of the progressive conservatives of the reign of Alexander I.

From *Sbornik Imperatorskogo Russkogo Istoricheskogo Obshchestva*, Vol. III (St. Petersburg: 1871), pp. 202-17.

The government of the state consists of eight main parts: (1) courts for the people, or justice; (2) rights of property, i.e., patrimonial affairs; (3) religious law and public mores, [i.e.,] what is

---

[1] Reprinted in E. S. Shumigorskii, *Imperator Pavel I—Zhizn' i tsarstvovanie* (St. Petersburg: 1907).

called internal policy; (4) foreign policy; (5) national defense; (6) state treasury affairs, i.e., the rate and quality of the currencies, the total amount of species in circulation in the state, all state revenues, and estimates of expenditures; (7) the economy of the state with respect to the preservation and increase of the population and of agriculture; (8) crafts, factories, manufactures, trade, and matters concerning merchants and townspeople.

Each of these main parts has many subdivisions, whose interconnection produces new and special areas, and everything together is administered through such offices as colleges, chancelleries, bureaus, and others, under whatever name. They all are under the direction of the Senate, which is like a center to which everything converges; being under the monarch's sovereign power, however, Senate may not have legislative power; it only administers in accordance with prescribed laws and statutes promulgated at different times, and in most cases perhaps, at the wrong time, i.e., when compelled by force of circumstances. Consequently, whatever its instructions to make use of the normal change in time and circumstances for the advantage of the state, the Senate, by virtue of its basic character, cannot follow them, for its first duty is to supervise the flow of current business and to make decisions based on the laws and decrees which regulate every administrative office. As a result, if one may be bold to say it, the Senate frequently takes harmful decisions based on laws which have been issued at different periods, sometimes hastily, sometimes inconsiderately, sometimes in prejudiced manner . . . , often not taking into account the fact that intervening circumstances and changes which have taken place in the state might—and sometimes in fact do—undermine the laws. From this it may be seen that if this [system] were followed consistently, not only would the Senate transcend its bounds, but the flow of business in the administration of the state would often come to a halt; instead of quick decisions there would be endless arguments and quarrels concerning new laws, not to mention the fact that physical and moral conditions inherent in such a numerous assembly do not allow for a discussion of legislation, but only for its scrutiny, even though, for other reasons to be mentioned below, such an assembly is nonetheless needed and useful.

The same basic conditions mean that all the business of the

areas of government mentioned above is taken care of in the respective colleges and bureaus with more regard to their conformity to office procedures than to their true success and general usefulness, for each office is bound by its own statutes which determine the distribution of business among them. But whoever thinks that the Governing Senate, by encompassing all [government] affairs, compensates for this defect is quite in error, because, as proven above, the Senate must act within the framework of the statutes of each office. The natural and necessary consequence of this [state of affairs] is that every senator and judge has no other aim than to render decisions provided for by the decrees and to submit a report on whatever is in doubt. Man's predisposition to laziness and idleness reinforces this pattern, as proven in everyday practice. Indeed, anyone who adheres strictly to his duties believes that he has adequately fulfilled them when on prescribed days he has been in attendance [at the office]; there, among the procurators and secretaries, he hopes to find a sufficient knowledge and understanding of the laws which are reported to him at the meeting and on the basis of which he has to make decisions. Naturally, such an official does not even spend an hour a day in examining the laws, decrees, and business personally, and in evaluating the good or harm that might come from them. And thus a senator, or any other official, arrives at the meetings like the guest to a dinner, who not only does not yet know the food's taste, but not even the dishes which he will be served. It would be a sin to condemn these people, for it is only to this [activity] that they have been called. Such is the nature of all offices in all states. And those who transcend these limitations are everywhere considered unusual, and their number, especially in the colleges, is also quite small everywhere.

From this, and especially from the autocracy's power of legislation, it may be naturally inferred that the principal, genuine, and over-all concern for the whole state resides in the person of the sovereign. But he cannot translate this concern into useful action, except by intelligently apportioning it among a small number of persons specially selected for this purpose.

Those who do not enter into the heart of things, but judge them only on the strength of their superficial appearance, are also wrong . . . in maintaining that the sovereign can find in the presidents of the colleges[2] and in the Procurator General of the Senate the particular concern for general [policy] matters which cannot exist in the individual members of these institutions. Excluding the three major colleges for Foreign Affairs, War, and Admiralty as being in nearly all respects separate from general domestic affairs, we must consider the colleges of Justice, Patrimonial affairs, Trade, Treasury, Mining, Manufacturing, Comptrol, and also the Office of Finance [*shtats kontora*], the Magistrate Office, and the Police. Their character and conditions have been sufficiently explained above. When they thus mutually undermine one another, even in matters taken up in the Senate, how can their presidents be concerned with matters of general interest? And if there should be such an exceptional person, it would not be by virtue of his office, but because of his special talents; consequently, such a person would transcend the confines of his office. To this may also be added [the consideration] that, if three or four [such] persons are hard to find, it is still more difficult to find nine or ten.

True, if the simple wording of a decree clearly decided a matter, the Procurator General might be considered such a general supervisor to whom everything is entrusted.[3] In his instruction he is called the Sovereign's eye; but as the Autocratic Sovereign, reserving to himself the right of legislation, obviously cannot survey through one eye the different administrative needs of the state which arise from changing times and circumstances, the Procurator General essentially is only the eye overseeing the regular flow of business and the accurate application of the laws in the Senate. We may agree that Iaguzhinskii[4] and Trubetskoi[5] extended their office much farther, but it should be noted that the former was at the time the closest adviser to the very Monarch who was then in the

---

[2] The presidents were ranking members of the boards which had constituted the central executive and administrative institutions of the Empire since Peter the Great.

[3] The duties of Procurator General of the Senate were defined by the act of 27 April 1722 (PSZ, No. 3979, "O dolzhnosti general prokurora").

[4] Count Pavel Ivanovich Iaguzhinskii (1683-1736): Procurator General of the Senate under Peter I. Under Anne he became cabinet minister.

[5] Prince Nikita Iur'evich Trubetskoi (1699-1767): General Field Marshal, for twenty years Procurator General of the Senate; also President of the College of War.

process of establishing the Empire's government—it is well known with what kind of people and by what means. It is sufficient to recall in this connection that the vice-chancellor mounted the scaffold only to teach the new senators how to attend and discuss properly in the Senate. If we take the reign of Elizaveta Petrovna, in his first period of office Prince Trubetskoi was Procurator General by virtue of court favor, as an accidental personage; consequently he did not enforce the laws and good order, but could and did everything and, we daresay, arbitrarily corrupted everything; in the later period he himself became the toady of favorites and minions.

This reign deserves special attention: during it everything was subordinated to the present moment, to the wishes of favorites, and to all the superficial and petty aspects of public affairs. Before that time our Monarchs already had had special high institutions; although these institutions had previously changed their form and location, the persons appointed to them had been given ranks and promotions to distinguish them from minions, and the Monarchs had still retained ways and means for paying attention to general matters of state, especially to those which by their very nature require constant correction, frequent changes, and useful innovations —all that cannot be taken care of out of the monarch's sight by ordinary institutions restricted both in the making and interpretation of the laws. The manner in which the late Empress came to the throne required of her, at least in the beginning, a reasoned policy in order to conform as much as possible to her great sire's incomplete statutes of government.[6] As a result, the Cabinet was immediately abolished—that Cabinet which had received its full form earlier and which, particularly after Biron's fall, had enabled the Monarch to have general care of all matters. Her Majesty remembered that her sovereign father had had a private cabinet from which nothing issued but particular decrees, orders, and letters, and she ordered the establishment of a similar cabinet for herself. The favorites and minions of the moment took advantage of this private

---

[6] Elizabeth seized the throne by overthrowing the regency of Anna Leopoldovna and her German advisers. She claimed to have taken only the rightful inheritance of her father Peter the Great and pledged to continue his work; hence her abolition of the Cabinet of Ministers, instituted by Empress Anne and the tool of the German favorites.

institution for the satisfaction of their own whims and interests, and by means of it they created a gap between the Monarch and the government—a situation that is always harmful to the common weal. These favorites and courtiers transformed this secret and unofficial institution into, as it were, a nest for all their caprices, and thereby the institution became the source of greatest harm, not only to the state but also to the sovereign. It was harmful to the state because, under the guise of imperial decrees and orders to all [governmental] institutions, it was the source of all the surprises and deceptions which corrupted the state's justice, laws, good order, and welfare. It was harmful to the Monarch himself because those very same people who used such underhand methods to hide themselves from the public tried particularly hard to blame on the monarch's own arbitrariness everything they themselves did in this manner; for a person entrusted with the business of a secret and basically unofficial institution may consider himself not subject to the judgment of the public and responsible to it, and consequently free from all obligations toward the monarch and the state. The flatterers, however, say to the sovereign: "But you have your Cabinet—command through it." This is a dangerous distinction! Do not all governmental institutions belong equally to the autocratic monarch if the whole state is his? The only difference, though, is that when the monarch's business comes from these governmental institutions, the public ascribes every surprise and error to the sovereign's ministers who, as officials, have a special obligation to prevent these from happening; and the ministers themselves cannot arrogantly shift the burden onto the monarch, for by virtue of their rank and office they are obliged to render account of their behavior not only to their sovereign but also to the public. On the other hand, a monarch who is always trusted and loved cannot be suspected by the people that, on his own (without the perfidious advice of others), he will prefer what is harmful to what is good. On the contrary, every good and useful matter is credited to the account of the sovereign's glory because it is to this end that he uses his intelligence, discrimination, will, and choice.

Under these circumstances, the state was in truth deprived of general governmental supervision, and only the routine flow of business was taken care of on the basis of various *ad hoc* decrees.

The sovereign was remote from government. Capricious favorites abused the Cabinet, corrupting the form and good order of government; from everywhere business was transferred to the Cabinet, and the Cabinet's prejudiced decrees and orders resulted in the matters never being fully settled. But even this was not enough: the favorites created a new institution, stranger than the first, by which general *aides-de-camp* on duty disposed of civilian posts; they created their own governmental procedures and ruled through them; illegally and without cause they intervened in matters concerning inheritances and the splitting up of individual private properties they had put under seal; they confiscated from one and gave to the other. All the while the dignitaries and favorites knew no limit to their aspirations and designs, though governmental plans remained unattended; everything was thrown into confusion; the most important duties and offices were transformed into ranks and rewards for favorites and flatterers; favor and seniority became everywhere the basis for assignments; nothing was left to talent and merit. The whims and favors of court intrigues enabled everyone to grab and take possession of the section of government he expected to be of greatest convenience in defeating his rival or for combining with others against a third.

If besides this arbitrariness there still remained some rules of [regular] government, they were, of course, of the kind that sacrificed the state's domestic prosperity for the sake of foreign affairs and which . . . precipitated a war[7] at the very moment when fearlessness, corruption, plunder, luxury, extravagance, and dissoluteness had reached their highest point. . . .

It was seen that a sudden war required real resources. It became necessary to gather in one center the scattered elements constituting the state and its administration. A Conference, a monster that looked like nothing, was set up: nothing was provided in it, and, consequently, everything was left to irresponsibility; and having wrested from the Sovereign a law to the effect that edicts signed by the Conference would compel execution everywhere, they [the favorites] cut off the Monarch from all business of state and, consequently, also from knowledge of their activities. To an enlightened

---

[7] The Seven Years' War.

ruler what matters is not the bold word but the word of truth. The favorite remained the life-giving or destructive element in the state; swept by the wind of inconstancy, without working, she only satisfied her whims; work and cares she turned over to the arrogant Volkov.[8] The latter, under the pretext of administering a bureaucratic order which did not exist, in fact performed the functions of prime minister; he ruled the ministers themselves, selected and decided affairs on his own, and forced the ministers to ratify them, invoking either the name of the Sovereign or—under cover of Her will—the favorite's wishes. Caprice was the only rule in selecting business for decision. Nor could it be otherwise when the areas of government were not separated in the highest institution of the state and when none was anybody's particular concern.

Most gracious Lady, this is the true essence of our governmental system, or rather of its absence; and this is the truthful picture of the results of the reign of the late humane Empress Elizaveta Petrovna.

Bolstered by knowledge, Your Majesty's perspicacity will no doubt perceive the dangers to Her autocracy stemming from the perfidious ideas of ill-wishers; under the pretext of [expressing] Your own will, they would deprive You of the power to bring about the country's good according to Your wish. Can a private proprietor manage his household if he does not first subdivide and organize it on an orderly basis? And how will an able manufacturer set up his factory if he assigns his master craftsmen to various machines and tasks on the basis of his liking of them, rather than according to their skill? Our master cobbler does not confuse the worker with the apprentice and hires each for the appropriate task. On the other hand, from people close to the throne I have had occasion to hear presented as a rule of statecraft the sycophantic proverb that "provided there is favor, anyone can take care of anything." Of course, this is what was practiced: the favors and rewards [granted] to individuals were transformed into a [public] trust that logically should have belonged only to those who possessed some specific knowledge and talent. On the one hand, this may be called forcing nature,

---

[8] Dmitrii Vasil'evich Volkov (1718-85): senator, Conference Secretary under Elizabeth, and Privy Secretary of the Particular Council under Peter III.

which, however, cannot be overcome; on the other, it finally compels moderate people to withdraw from regular matters commensurate with their talents and to put their efforts into obtaining chance favors. From this springs the natural consequence that affairs fall behind, while the intrigues of factions are in full swing.

It is salutary for our much suffering fatherland that Your Majesty's motherly intention is to make use of the full autocratic power entrusted to You by God and the people to establish a system and secure an order of government such as to enable Your Majesty always to promote your Empire's just and general interests and welfare.

In fulfillment of the command Your Imperial Majesty has given me, I hereby humbly submit a project in the form of an act for Your Majesty's signature. My most humble loyalty and devotion to the sacred person of Your Majesty, a genuine love for Your glory, and a disinterested zeal for my fatherland were my only rules in seeking out and in formulating such statutes of monarchic government which . . . could produce, as a result of Your long reign, the age of Catherine the Great, surpassing in its excellence that of all your predecessors on the Russian throne.

I dare to flatter myself, most gracious Lady, that this project —which establishes the form of the highest state institution for legislation from which, as from a single Sovereign and a single place, there will issue forth the Monarch's own decision—will give life to everything and protect the autocratic power from its secret destroyers. No less do I hope that in it Your Imperial Majesty will deign to recognize the usefulness and essential need for departments and ministries.

Concerning the division of the Senate into departments, everybody recognizes its advantages for the speedier flow of business. For my part, I also see in it reasons of state policy of even greater importance for the Empire. For over thirty years we have experienced palace revolutions, and the more their force is spread among commoners, the more daring, safe, and feasible they become. Among Your Imperial Majesty's wise measures to cope with a situation fraught with danger for the future, attention should also be paid to the fact that by increasing the number of senators greater respect will be shown to the government, and the Senate in turn will thereby be astrained to the order of the state.

Most gracious Lady, besides fulfilling in this manner my duty and manifesting the obedience which behooves a most loyal subject, I should in all humility remark to Your Imperial Majesty that, as she knows, there are among us persons to whom such a new organization of the government would be undesirable because of considerations of private interest known only to them. For this reason Your Imperial Majesty should not consider this business completed for the good of the people merely by giving her consent to this or some other project; it will require Your Imperial Majesty's care and firmness, so that Your Majesty's Council will acquire immediately its proper form and may be brought into action; indeed, in the beginning, most gracious Lady, there is almost no possible doubt that these personages will endeavor to find difficulties in its establishment or, as a last resort, will try to shape it the way they themselves would wish for. In such a case, it is immeasurably more useful to establish [the form] now, rather than, as has been the case in the past, to allow the corruption of what has been established. Having said this, I am unto my grave, Your Imperial Majesty's [most humble slave].

*Manifesto on the Establishment*
*of an Imperial Council*
*and on the Division of the*
*Senate into Departments*

By the Grace of God, We, Catherine II, Empress and Autocrat of All Russia, etc., etc., etc.

Long before acceding to the Russian throne, having gained knowledge of the nature of the government of this great and powerful Empire, we have also learned of the causes which so frequently and under varying circumstances have resulted in a neglect of the affairs of the state; i.e., the weakness of justice for the people, the neglect of the people's welfare, and lastly, all those vices which in course of time have taken root throughout the entire administration; and more particularly, how at the accession of the late Empress Anna Ioannovna, the autocratic power itself, which had never been separated from our imperial crown, was already shaken.[9]

Such occurrences harmful to the state were doubtlessly caused in part by the fact that government business was determined rather by the influence of individual personalities than by the power of the state institutions. In part, though, [the harmful effects were caused] by an absence of such principles which could firmly preserve the organizational form of the government.

Our intention—worthy of our Imperial Majesty—and our motherly concern for the secure welfare of our Empire compel us to give our own estimate of the inadequacies of our glorious ancestors' political statutes.

The short life, burdened by difficulties and wars, of the Great Peter, the creator and legislator of the Russian Empire, our beloved grandfather,[10] did not allow him to complete the civil political establishment; his successors on the Russian throne, viewing the mere foundations laid by him as if they were the forms of government, endeavored to take care of the defects noticed by them by various temporary regulations and legislations. In the absence of a firm foundation in the state, however, and lacking the force of permanence, the latter either lapsed of themselves as times changed, or fell under the control of accidental favorites. So that even the highest institutions of our autocratic government were preserved only in name, while the entire state was governed by ignorant individuals and their pleasure, outside [the framework] of institutions.

Institutions which from the beginning had been inadequate, after a time and as a result of frequent abuses, have brought the administration of our beloved fatherland to such a pass that even when the most important events were taking place on the Monarch's throne it was considered superfluous and unnecessary to con-

---

[9] The accession crisis of 1730 and the "conditions" imposed on Anne by the Supreme Privy Council (see Chapter I above).

[10] Peter III, husband of Catherine II, was the grandson of Peter the Great through his mother Anne. Following in the footsteps of Elizabeth, Catherine II was eager to identify herself with the reign and work of Peter the Great.

voke the highest institutions of government. What loyal and reasonable son of the fatherland can recall without emotion the manner in which the former Emperor Peter III ascended the throne? And does not such an unfortunate situation belong rather to those times when not only was there no established government, but not even written laws?

It is an unquestioned truth that time, experience, and skill are the most reliable witnesses to good and evil. Observing and thinking about their effects for several years, we have perceived the advantage that successors naturally have over their ancestors, and this is particularly true for rulers. That is why, at the very moment of our accession to the throne, we have assumed before God and our people the imperial obligation that with the help of the Almighty, under His Holy guidance, and with our autocratic power, we will correct the defects in the administration of our Empire mentioned above and remedy the harm that on occasion stems from them; in short, to secure on an indestructible basis the forms and procedures by which—under imperial autocratic power—the state will always be governed; all this we have solemnly promised to our beloved subjects in the lengthy Manifesto of July 6th of this year.[11] We have based ourselves particularly on those words of the Spiritual Regulations of 1721,[12] signed by all the Holy Council and Synod and confirmed by the autocratic hand of our grandfather, the *Sovereign Lord,* Peter the Great, in which this glorious and wise ruler says: the power of monarchs is autocratic, God Himself commands to obey them for conscience's sake; and [the monarchs] have their counselors not only to learn the truth better, but also so that disobedient men may not slanderously say that the monarch has commanded such and such by force and out of caprice, rather than [guided] by justice and truth.

And thus, by virtue of the power given to us by God for the

---

[11] "Manifesto of 6 July 1762": the reference is actually to the manifesto of 7 July 1762 (PSZ, No. 11598), issued on the occasion of the coronation of Catherine II and justifying her seizure of power at greater length than did the manifesto of her accession of 28 June 1762 (PSZ, No. 11582).

[12] *Dukhovnyi Reglament,* 25 January 1721 (PSZ, No. 3718): drafted by Feofan Prokopovich, established the new Church administration and defined the duties of the Holy Synod.

protection of our Empire against harm and for the purpose of extending genuine well-being to our true sons, we most solemnly hereby establish and legislate the following statute for our high government institution:

1. We command and establish an Imperial Council. It is to have six *and up to eight members,* who are to be called Imperial Councilors, and their number should never exceed *eight* or fall *below six.*

2. Included in this number should be a few State Secretaries from the departments of government and [who] consequently have a seat in these departments, such as: (1) the State Secretary for Foreign Affairs and member of that department, i.e., the College of Foreign Affairs; (2) the State Secretary for Internal Affairs, who must not only be a Senator, but also have a seat in all those colleges which belong to that department; (3) the State Secretary of the War Department, who is to have a seat in the War College, the Commissariat and Quartermaster, and in the Corps of Artillery, Engineers, and Cadets; (4) the State Secretary of the naval department who is also a member of the Admiralty College. And if, because of the extent of its concerns, it shall be necessary to divide the department for internal affairs, then the fifth State Secretary ought to be added [to the Council] on a similar basis. . . .

4. All matters which on the basis of statutes and by virtue of our autocratic monarchic power fall within our own concern and decision—such as reports submitted to us outside the Senate, opinions, projects, all the petitions addressed to us, complete information on all the various aspects constituting the state's welfare—in short, everything that is to serve the autocrat personally in his efforts at increasing and improving the state is to be [taken up] in the Council as if it were by us personally.

5. //For the sake of convenience and efficiency, distribute the matters mentioned in article 4 among four departments, each headed by a State Secretary.// The Imperial Council is nothing but the institution in which we labor for the sake of the Empire; and, consequently, all matters coming to us as the Sovereign ought to be distributed according to their character among the State Secretaries; and the latter shall review them in their departments, work

them out, clarify them, submit them to us in Council, and dispose of them according to our decisions and orders.

6. . . . The establishment of this Imperial Council has and cannot have any other purpose than to enable the sovereign to extend his personal concern to all aspects of the state, in order to legislate for the best interests of the common weal. . . . //The Councilors should be energetic and strong, as well as talented and informed persons. To give the Sovereign greater range, ease, and freedom in selecting Councilors, the office carries no special rank.//

7, 8, 9. //Technical details of bureaucratic procedure.//

10. Every new legislation, act, decision, manifesto, charter, and letter patent which sovereigns sign themselves must be countersigned by the State Secretary in whose department it was prepared, so that the public may know to what department it pertains.

11. From the above it may be seen that nothing may issue from the Imperial Council except over the Monarch's own signature. . . .

Having established our imperial council in this manner, we shall now turn to those aspects of the procedures and organization of the Senate (without destroying its unity) which we deem necessary to elaborate for the sake of the nation's welfare.

1. Not only do we leave in its previous form the legislation on which this government institution is based, but in addition we confirm the right which our grandfather Peter the Great, the founder of this Governing body under the autocratic power, has recognized and granted to it, i.e., the right of making representations concerning even our own commands if their implementation touches upon or negatively affects the laws of the state or the welfare of our people. . . .[13]

2. In addition, the Senate should be subdivided into six departments: //(1) internal political affairs; (2) appellate department, petitions, heraldry; (3) affairs of the colleges for mines, trade, and manufactures, and of the Main Magistrate; (4) affairs of the colleges

---

[13] This reference is probably to article 9 of the decree of 27 April 1722 on the duties of the Senate (PSZ, No. 3978), in which the Senate's right of making representations (*droit de remontrance*) is alluded to in very vague terms.

of justice and patrimonies; (5) military and naval matters; (6) affairs concerning the Ukraine, Livonia, Estonia, New Serbia, Vyborg, Narva, and German matters//. This division is not inviolable and permanent and may be changed according to needs and circumstances.

5. //Decisions in the departments to be reached by unanimous vote.//

6. //In case of disagreement, the matter to be decided by the General Assembly of the Senate by majority vote.//

7, 8. //Technical details of organization.//

# III

# Memorandum of Prince Bezborodko Concerning the Needs of the Russian Empire (1799)

## Introduction

Scion of an old Ukrainian Cossack officer family, Aleksandr Andreevich Bezborodko (1749-99) rose to be Catherine II's virtual prime minister in the last years of her reign. Unlike most of her high dignitaries, he also managed to retain a measure of political influence under Paul I.

In the memorandum he wrote for Paul I shortly before his death, Bezborodko demonstrated a growing awareness of the need not merely to reform the structure of the administration and extend the role of the Senate as an organ of supervision and protection, but to strike at the social structure as well. Bezborodko thought primarily of transforming the main classes of Russian society into genuine estates. In his view such a transformation would guarantee security of person and property to the majority of the Russian autocrat's subjects. Bezborodko was even willing to face the problem of serfdom and to envisage its eventual, albeit very gradual, elimination.

From "Kniaz' Aleksandr Andreevich Bezborodko v sviazi
s sobytiiami svoego vremeni," by N. Grigorovich, in
*Sbornik Imperatorskogo Russkogo Istoricheskogo
Obshchestva*, Vol. XXIX (St. Petersburg: 1881), Appendix
No. 18, pp. 643-46.

Russia is an autocratic state. Its size, the variety of its inhabitants and customs, and many other considerations make it the only
natural form of government for Russia. All arguments to the contrary are futile, and the least weakening of autocratic power would
result in the loss of many provinces, the weakening of the state, and
countless misfortunes for the people.[1]

An autocratic sovereign, if he possesses the qualities befitting
his rank, must feel that he has been given unlimited power not to
rule according to his whim, but to respect and implement the laws
established by his ancestors and by himself; in short, having spoken
his law, he is himself the first to respect and obey it, so that others
may not even dare to think of evading or escaping it.

In Russia the throne is hereditary. The act promulgated at
the coronation of Paul I adequately explains the rules;[2] and provided it is strictly enforced, there can arise neither confusions nor
troubles.

The Russian Emperor must be of the Eastern Greek Orthodox
faith, and so must be his spouse, his heir, and the latter's spouse; as
for the spouses of other Russian grand dukes, however, they may be
of another Christian denomination; but no one should be invested
with [the right to] succession if he has not accepted the Orthodox
faith.

The Emperor's coronation is a rite by which the Sovereign
solemnly renders thanks to God, confesses his faith before the altar
and the people, and receives God's pledge of assistance for the better government of his realm. It would not go counter to his autocratic power if, after pronouncing the symbol of the creed, the

---

[1] This is an obvious allusion to the argument of Montesquieu (*Esprit
des Lois*, Livre VIII, chapitre 19, repeated by Catherine II in her *Nakaz*
(Chapter II, Nos. 9-12).

[2] Act of Succession and Statute of the Imperial Family, 5 April 1797 (PSZ,
No. 17906).

Monarch would give an oath which would clearly show to his people his intention to rule for the glory of the Empire and the welfare of the country. The oath could be as follows.[3]

In Russia there are three estates [*dostoianie*]: noblemen, burghers [*meshchanstvo*], peasants [*poselianin*]. The character and privileges of each are different, but their common traits consist of the following: (1) equal protection of the law for everyone; (2) equal security of person and property; (3) participation in administration according to the law established for them.

The privileges of the nobles are set forth in the Charter of 1785 and the provincial laws;[4] there is almost no need, therefore, to expand them, but merely to collect and order them.

In their Charter of 1785 and in various provincial rights,[5] the burghers, too, possess privileges that are sufficiently clear.

But the condition of the peasants is such as to require improvement. God forbid, I do not mean thereby the kind of excessive liberty which, under cover of this innocent name, would change into willfulness and give cause for the claims of a general and actually chimerical equality. What I mean here is this: it is undeniable that in Russia all lands belong as rightful property to landowners [*pomeshchik*]. The Monarch himself is the owner of his own estates, the lands of the crown, Economy lands,[6] state lands, and all the free [unused] land of his Empire. Consequently, no one may use land except under condition of some advantage [accruing] to its owner. These conditions may be voluntary or established by state law. From this it follows that the peasant or cultivator is obligated to compensate the owner either through payment of a due or by his labor, commensurate with the value of the land. Concerning labor obligations, there is no need to enter into great detail, but only repeat and clarify Paul I's manifesto of 5 April 1797 concerning peas-

---

[3] The present memorandum exists in draft form only, and the text of the oath is missing.

[4] Special privileges of the nobility in some border provinces, such as the Baltic lands, Ukraine, White Russia.

[5] This refers to the Magdeburg Law and similar customs still in force in some cities of the Empire.

[6] Secularized Church lands: see J. Blum, *Lord and Peasant in Russia from the Ninth to the Nineteenth Centuries* (Princeton, N.J.: Princeton University Press, 1962), p. 480.

ant labor.[7] As to quitrents [*obrok*], they ought to be left to agreement between landowners and peasants. But along with it, there should be promulgated the following articles in favor of the peasants: (1) The peasants must be attached to the land and belong to those persons under whose name (or under whose ancestor's name) they have been listed by the censuses. (2) Transfer from one village to another or to other lands cannot take place except with the knowledge of the administration and voluntarily. (3) Villages cannot be sold except together with their lands; the sale of individuals —which is true slavery—is to be forbidden, including sales on account of army recruits, for recruits should be drawn in the order decided upon by the village assembly. (4) All movables are the inalienable property of the peasant, and the landowner may not burden the [peasants'] capital in cash in excess of the amount obtained by the Emperor from [assessment of] the capital of merchants. (5) While the use of peasants for household services is unavoidable, provision should be made either for returning them to the plow or to have them replaced by others; or still provide for their freedom and the right, at the next census, to choose an occupation or status according to the terms of Catherine II's Manifesto of 17 March 1775.[8] In this manner the peasants' true freedom will come about; and when the lower [village] police courts and other institutions created by Catherine are re-established with the necessary improvements, the tranquillity of this estate will have been secured for a long time.

Until now, no corruption comparable to the false equality of the French had ever entered the heads of our lower classes, because everybody preferred to rise from low to high status on an individual basis. The freed-serf, or the state peasant, endeavored to become a merchant, and the rich merchant endeavored to become an official or nobleman. It is desirable that this drive remain strong, but its realization should be made more difficult in such a way as to bene-

---

[7] Paul's manifesto defined the number of days a serf had to work his lord's land; the decree was never successfully implemented (PSZ, No. 17909).

[8] Article 46 of the manifesto of 17 March 1775 (PSZ, No. 14275: "O Vysochaishe darovannykh raznym sosloviiam milostiiam po sluchaiiu zakliucheniia mira s Portoi Ottomanskoi").

fit the state: [continuing] payments of dues until the new census, taxes on capital, and some contribution to the town treasure on the part of those peasants who become merchants are most needed and profitable. Merit and great benefits publicly brought to the state would be decisive with respect to the [attainment of] nobility. . . .

The Governing Senate, established by Peter the Great, is the highest governmental institution in Russia. Privy Councilors and Actual Privy Councilors are members of the Senate. On ceremonial occasions they wear ermine-trimmed, red velvet capes and plumed hats, like the members of orders of chivalry.

The Senate is divided into the following departments: the first, which is in charge of political and executive affairs, publishes decrees, and in a word (copy from the Statute on the Provincial Administration and enlarge on it); the second is the criminal department; the third, the civil department; the fourth is concerned with Treasury affairs. The second and third departments may be subdivided into two or more; it would be desirable to have two of these departments in Moscow and two in Kiev.

The Presidents of the first three Colleges[9] sit in the Senate in three cases: (1) when the Emperor attends; (2) when a matter requiring the issuance of a general law is under discussion; (3) in case of a general criminal trial of supreme importance. All Governor-Generals sit in and have a voice in the Senate.

//Details on the Senate's organization and procedures.//

A Procurator General is to be established to safeguard the rights of the autocracy, the interests of the state, and the respect due to justice and the laws.

The office of State Jurist or Chancellor of Justice is established to stand guard over the power of the law.

For cases which exceed the scope of general rules and those in which humanitarian sentiment demands a mitigation of the laws, there is established a Supreme Court in Equity;[10] its president is the Chief Justice in Equity, and two deputies from the nobility, two from the burghers, and two from the peasants are its members.

---

[9] Foreign Affairs, War, Navy.
[10] *Vysshii Sovestnyi Sud.*

As the Sovereign cannot personally supervise such a vast empire, he does so through trusted persons; namely, one senator and two deputies from the nobility, two from the burghers, and two from the peasantry; and every province must be inspected by them in detail every three years.

A General Criminal Court is set up under the Senate's supervision; it consists of a president holding the second rank [*chin*], two members of fourth or fifth rank, and two deputies of the nobility, two from the burghers, and two from the peasantry. Cases and persons not subject to the jurisdiction of the provincial courts are tried in this court.

The general assembly of the deputies [on the courts], under the presidency of the Chancellor of Justice, supervises the laws of the state; it consists of four councilors of the fourth and fifth ranks. When a new law is issued, its draft proposal is sent for consideration to this assembly, then for general review to the plenary assembly of the Senate, and lastly it is confirmed by the Autocrat.

If on its first reading in the Senate a decree will seem to be harmful, the Senate has the right to make a unanimous representation to the Sovereign; but if the latter reiterates his will, it is registered and implemented without further representations.

Criminal cases involving capital punishment cannot, of course, be completed without presentation to the Sovereign. The latter, while giving full freedom to the natural course of justice, has the power, by show of his mercy, to forgive the guilty or to alleviate his punishment.

//Procedures for crimes of *lèse-majesté;* definition restricted to the cases enumerated in the *Nakaz* of Catherine II.//

In the investigation of these cases [of *lèse-majesté*], all secret procedure is abolished, and so are those practices which abusively shed the blood of men and citizens, despite the provisions of the laws applicable in other criminal cases.

Although all decisions of the Senate are to be implemented, decisions involving the deprivation of a nobleman of his honor will not be carried out without prior report to the Sovereign.

# IV

## Project for a Most Graciously Granted Charter to the Russian People (1801)

### Introduction

The assassination of Paul I and the accession of Alexander I had been engineered by a group of high officials and courtiers exasperated (as well as frightened) by the threat to the nobility's security of person and property which Paul's pathological capriciousness and tyranny had created. There was, therefore, a strong urge to initiate such steps as would prevent the repetition of the kind of arbitrary and cruel rule witnessed under Paul. The promise made by Alexander I to reign in the spirit of his grandmother, Catherine II, who had laid the foundations for the nobility's corporate autonomy, encouraged leading dignitaries to believe that they could secure Alexander's formal approval to a document that would set forth the fundamental rights of Russia's upper classes.

One such proposal of a charter of basic rights for all of the Emperor's free subjects, to be made public at the coronation of Alexander I, was drafted in the circle of the brothers Alexander and Simon Vorontsov. The exact authorship of the Charter has not been determined. We do know that it was the work of several hands; in particular, it reflected the thinking of Count Alexander Romanovich Vorontsov (1741-1805), who became Chancellor. The participation, at least in a technical capacity, of Alexander Radishchev and M. M. Speransky has been established, though their specific contribution to the final product is still a matter of dispute.

The basic personal rights of the free subjects of the Empire set forth in the Charter are, quite clearly, modeled on the legal safeguards enjoyed by contemporary English gentlemen. But, in addition, the authors of the Charter were much concerned to protect private property against the government's arbitrary actions and safeguard the basic means for economic activity—more particularly, those of the peasantry. In the final analysis, the Charter aimed at defining, as clearly and as completely as was possible under Russian conditions, the area within which the individual's person and activity would be protected and secured by law.

From *Radishchev—ocherki i issledovaniia*
by V. P. Semennikov (Moscow-Petrograd: 1923), pp. 180-94.

In announcing to our beloved and loyal subjects our accession to our ancestors' throne by will of the Almighty, in a manifesto[1] issued the same day we stated our will and resolution to use all our strength and endeavor to make Russia happy by governing the people, entrusted by God to our rule, on the basis of fundamental laws, and by keeping as our primary aim the welfare of all our loyal subjects; we shall endeavor to perform this duty dear to our heart to the fullest extent; and to God we offer our warm prayers that He may strengthen us and help us in carrying the burden of this service He has imposed on us.

On the occasion of our coronation and anointment, before God who sees all hearts and before the illustrious and numerous peoples under our scepter, we deem it our duty to declare that our

---

[1] Manifesto of accession in which Alexander I promised to rule in the spirit of his grandmother, Catherine II.

first and only goal will always be the welfare, peace, and integrity of the Russian state and nation. For ourselves, we take as a rule the truth that it is not the people who have been made for the Monarchs, but it is the Monarchs who have been established by Divine Providence for the benefit and welfare of the peoples living under their rule; and to this end we decree and promise on our imperial word, for ourselves and our heirs, the following articles as the fundamental law:

1. Recognizing the extent of the inadequacy of existing laws, to the improvement of which our predecessors have already given thought, we consider it to be our duty to direct our particular attention to this important subject. To this end we have already established a special commission,[2] as we wish nothing more than to see the success of our purpose of having Russia acquire new strength and happiness by means of adequate and clear laws for all regions and all estates which make up our vast Empire; so that everybody's personal security and property is protected, and that, if there must be punishments, they should be determined only by the nature of the crime, and that no one's life be burdened with a burden greater than his wrongdoing. We shall experience genuine satisfaction only when we see our country endowed with all the laws necessary to provide for its general welfare, in such a manner that everybody may live under their protection in peace and security during our reign and during that of our successors.

2. We confirm and renew all rights and privileges granted to the nobility by previous Russian Monarchs, and more specifically by the decree of Peter III entitled "On the liberties of the nobility" and the Charter of the Nobility of Empress Catherine II.

3. We confirm and give to the members of the nobility full freedom to reside in whatever part of the Russian Empire they wish, to change their residence, to leave the country, and to return to their country, as they will decide; not in the least afraid that by leaving the confines of Russia their estates or rights might be jeopardized or violated, for they will remain under the protection of the laws safeguarding property. The freedom to travel beyond

---

[2] Alexander I ordered that a Commission on Laws be established to prepare a new code of laws (25 August 1801, PSZ, No. 19989).

the borders of the state should be the inviolate right of a Russian nobleman, and for whose exercise he need not request the Monarch's permission each time, except in extraordinary circumstances, e.g., break of relations with a power or something similar, which, however, will always be made known publicly.

4. The Russian nobleman shall have the freedom to enter or not to enter our service; but those who do not perform any kind of service cannot enjoy the advantages and privileges acquired by dint of service. It is our will, however, that those noblemen who for various reasons cannot fulfill this duty [of service] to the fatherland, and are deprived of the advantages and privileges acquired through it, still enjoy the rights which naturally belong to every nobleman who possesses real estate, [namely] the right to elect and be elected to the offices which depend on election by the nobility.

The Russian noblemen shall be free to enter the service of friendly or allied powers without having to request special permission to do so.

5. The order of succession and the rights of inheritance shall remain unshakeable and inviolate under the laws of the Russian Empire; and the order of succession established by law shall never, under any circumstance, be abrogated or violated by any power whatsoever; and all special regulations which undermine this order (as, for example, a confirmed testament, a petition confirmed by His Imperial Majesty, or any other change in the legally established rule) shall have no [legal] force . . . from now on and forever.

The general rule with regard to the inheritance of real estate, which has for long been recognized as the law, states that: while every Russian subject who owns property disposes of his patrimonial or inherited estate according to the terms of Russian law, he may give away or freely will his acquired property as he sees fit.

6. The domestic and foreign trade of the Russian Empire shall always and at all times enjoy the special protection of the government; [the latter] shall give its unstinted attention to increasing the production of natural and manufactured articles in the state; and incentive shall be given to the prospecting of all useful items, such as iron ores, minerals, salt, and other products of the soil.

Any owner who has acquired and found on his property the aforementioned products of the soil that are so useful to the state and to the expansion of trade shall have permanent and unquestioned title to them, wherever these products may have been found —on the surface or in the earth's bowels, in forests, water, or anywhere on his property; and he shall have the right to process them for his own benefit; and except for taxes set by law, the Treasury shall have no other claims whatsoever.

It is the duty of the government to see to it that everywhere in the realm there shall be available all the means possible for the transportation and carting of any natural or manufactured products; it shall protect and give every possible assistance in the exchange and production of goods; and no one shall ever have to fear that a barrier might be put to this internal circulation under any pretext whatever, or that it might be hamstrung by any regulation or legislation which would preclude or impede the general good in such an important area. And any statutes presently in force, or which possibly might come into existence at some future time, shall be invalid if they are barriers to the attainment of this goal that is so useful for the welfare of the people.

7. We confirm and proclaim irrevocably and forever that personal security is a right which naturally belongs to every Russian subject; everyone, therefore, shall enjoy it in accordance with his title and rank. This right shall remain forever under the sacred protection of the law.

We renew, confirm, and decree that the right to movable and real property is a right enjoyed by a Russian subject to the extent set forth by law for every estate of the realm.

8. Every Russian subject shall enjoy unhindered freedom of thought, creed or religion, worship, speech, writing, and action, to the extent that these are not contrary to the laws of the state and not damaging to anyone else.

9. By virtue of the decree of 1787 we confirm the right of civil prescription regarding ownership or possession of movable or real property. . . .[3]

---

[3] Article 4 of the manifesto of 28 June 1787 (PSZ, No. 16551: "O raznykh darovannykh narodu milostiam").

Peaceful and unchallenged possession for ten years, confirmed by right of prescription or expiration, shall be transformed
into a right to actual and unchallenged ownership, and it shall
serve in lieu of a legal and documentary title, if the latter is not
available.

10. We confirm and renew all the rights and privileges given
by Russian Monarchs to cities, merchants, and townspeople, and in
particular by the Charter of Her Majesty, Empress Catherine II,
called the Statute of the Towns.[4]

11. We confirm and grant to all those entered on the rosters of
merchants and townspeople the freedom to choose and change their
residence in all towns, as they wish. Likewise they shall be free to
travel abroad, [though] reliable security will be required of those
who have some obligations [pending], and also to ensure the regular
payment of taxes due by them.

12. If in settlement of some claim, or for whatever other
reason, the land of a peasant becomes subject to distraint, confiscation, or seizure, no agricultural implements and no things
appertaining to his calling—such as hoe, plow, or harrow, scythe,
cart, etc., horses, oxen, granary with seed grain, barn or threshing
barn, and all other agricultural buildings—shall be taken away
under any pretext at any time.

This property on which the peasant's condition is based cannot be violated under any guise or pretext, be it in payment of a
debt to the Treasury, as penalty for tax arrears, for taxes due, or for
any claim by the [land] owner; and it shall remain sacred and inviolate forever. For, deprived of it, the peasant is deprived of his
way of life.

13. No one accused of a crime or under trial shall be considered to be a criminal and deprived of his good name in society;
and he is to enjoy all personal privileges (if he has any) until it has
been truly proven that he has committed the crime and [this fact]
made known by the definitive sentence of lawful judges.

14. On our Imperial word we promise to give all our attention
to improve the law (in part already in force in Russian jurispru-

---

[4] 21 April 1785 (PSZ, No. 16188).

dence) that every Russian subject is equal in status to his judges.[5] Nothing will be more pleasing to our heart than to see in our Empire the firm establishment of justice based on solid rules, the same for all estates.

15. //Right to counsel for the accused.//

16. A person accused or under trial has the inviolable right to recuse the judges appointed to sit in trial over him, provided he makes known the lawful cause for his recusation.

The recusation of judges ought to apply equally to civil cases.

17. No one not empowered by law shall dare violate the personal security of any Russian subject (of whatever estate) by depriving him of his freedom, by imprisoning him, by putting him in fetters, or even by keeping him under guard.

18. Anyone arrested or put in jail or detained anywhere by force, who in the course of three days has not been informed of the cause for which he has been arrested, put in jail, or detained, and who, in the course of these three days, has not been brought before a lawful court for the purpose of being questioned and given a trial, shall be freed immediately (merely upon his demand) by the nearest authorities, because his crime is still unknown, and does not, therefore, have any existence in law.

He who has been freed in this manner may sue, for injury to his personal security and for damages, the person who has arrested him, or put him in jail, or detained him, or given orders to that effect.

19. //Right to be released on bail, except in enumerated cases of capital crimes or by decision of the court. Cases of *lèse-majesté* to be clearly defined on the basis of Chapter XX of the *Nakaz* of Catherine II, so that they may not serve as pretext for arbitrary interpretation or excuse—the main categories here are acts, preparation, and conspiracy to rebellion, overthrow of the government, treason, attentate against the Emperor's person.//

20. //A Russian subject shall not be put in double jeopardy.//

21. In the event of a court examination or suit between the Treasury and a private person, the Treasury shall not be considered in court otherwise than an ordinary defendant or plaintiff. The

---

[5] An allusion to trial by jury of peers.

attorney defending the rights of the Treasury shall have no privilege
or preference over his opponent, and with respect to the Treasury
all those forms, procedures, and sequences are to be observed which
are established for private persons; for the status and privileges of
either plaintiff or defendant should not have the least influence on
the procedures followed in collecting evidence or in conducting
the trial, and especially not on decisions or sentences. All persons
are equally subject to the law.

22. From now on there shall be no tax, duty, collection of
monies or anything else, nor any requisition without an imperial
decree to that effect. [In this decree] the tax, duty, collection, or
requisition shall be set forth clearly, and it shall be promulgated
on a nation-wide basis in Our name by the Governing Senate; and
in this promulgation there will be indicated clearly, understand-
ably, and unambiguously what is required of whom, and in what
amount.

This protective measure shall abolish all private exactions or
taxes levied by any authorities such as town administrations,
magistracies, *ratushas* [town police and tax courts], guild boards,
assemblies, or marshals of the nobility, or by others. The power
and right to levy taxes in accordance with His Imperial Majesty's
will shall belong exclusively to the Governing Senate. This rule
does not preclude voluntary contributions or collections by noblemen, merchants, burghers, guilds, or state peasants for the benefit
of their particular estate. Such voluntary contributions or collection should not be made without prior consultation of all participants.

23. Punishments provided by law can have only two aims:
either to rehabilitate the criminal or to prevent crimes by the example of punishment; it is therefore unnatural that the government
find any profit therein, for the fines or penalties set by law in various
instances of civil procedure must always aim at correcting the
criminals by depriving them of the pretext for crime. In criminal
cases which entail civil death there ought to be no fines or dep-
rivations of property, for the consequences of this punishment
[deprivations of property] fall on the heirs; therefore, we decree
that henceforth, in criminal cases, there shall be no confiscation of
property for the benefit of the Treasury. If under provision of the

law, therefore, the guilty is sentenced to civil death, his property shall be given to his lawful heirs on the basis of the normal order of succession, and it passes on hereditarily according to regular and lawful procedure.

//Exception: in case the criminal has caused a loss either to the Treasury or to a private person, the financial claims against him must first be satisfied out of his property.//

24. In all court examinations or trials, property and person have to be distinguished and separated. In cases of real action and litigation, the person or the individual, whatever his family, may be subject to response, penalty, or claim only when the object or property prove inadequate to the satisfaction of the claim.

In consequence of this rule, the law states that any kind of transactions such as sale, hire, agreement, contract, loan, settlement, or obligation of whatever type, either between private persons or between the Treasury and private persons, are acts pertaining not to the individual undertaking the obligation but to the object with respect to which the obligation is undertaken; such acts involve not persons but property. Consequently, the property or object are first answerable for keeping the promises and fulfilling the obligations; but, if the property is insufficient to satisfy the obligations that have been assumed, the law then turns to the individual or person, so that he may make up for the lack of property in satisfaction of the claim.

25. Wishing to consolidate the right of private property in all its respects and forms, we relinquish the Treasury's claims to the property of the last member of a family; and we decree that, henceforth, such individuals may dispose of their property according to rights common to all owners, and they shall have the power to mortgage, to sell, or to dispose of it in any other lawful manner; only those properties shall be considered escheats and revert to the Treasury for which the owners (being without heirs) have made no disposition in their lifetime and have died intestate. [Procedural technical details] [6]

---

[6] This provision is related to the efforts made by prominent members of the upper rungs of the nobility to introduce some form of primogeniture and entail in Russia to limit the effects of the division of estates at every generation.

26. Having provided as much as possible for the security of our loyal subjects, we consider that their happiness will depend very much on whether judicial procedures, in whatever case, are given clear and permanent foundations by statute. Until such time when, with God's help, we achieve our goal of securing Russia's happiness by the draft and publication of a general code, we promise on our imperial word that we shall scrupulously abide by all the judicial procedures or regulations which have been enacted to this date, without abrogating any through general or particular statutes. But in case previous regulations, procedures, or judicial proceedings should need some amending, in every instance . . . the Governing Senate shall examine in detail the amendments that have to be made in the existing statutes; to this end [the Senate] shall hold a general consultation, inviting to it the colleges and other government offices of equal status; and, having considered [the matter], draft the statute and present it to us for confirmation. Only then shall such a new statute have force of law, while everything enacted in a different way shall be legally invalid.

# V

## Principles of Government Reform
## (of the Unofficial Committee, 1802)

### Introduction

To make good on the promise given in his manifesto of accession to bring some order to the "chaotic structure of the Empire," Emperor Alexander I surrounded himself with a small group of friends who were to help him work out the principles of necessary reforms. The group, meeting informally and almost secretly, was dubbed the Unofficial Committee and consisted of Count Paul A. Stroganov (1772-1817), Count Victor P. Kochubei (1768-1834), Nicholas N. Novosil'tsev (1761-1836), and Prince Adam A. Czartoryski (1770-1861). Stroganov was most active in submitting ideas on the method and direction to be followed by the Committee in its work.

The ultimate goal of the members of the Committee is not too easy to formulate, for much remained pretty vague, and contradictory viewpoints were never reconciled. In general, we may infer that their final aim was not unlike the aspiration expressed in the Charter to the Russian People. The main difference was one of method. The Unofficial Committee wanted the work of reform to be initiated and implemented by officials of the autocracy, without the participation of the "estates." Public opinion was to enter the picture only to the extent that its free expression would provide the government with much-needed information on conditions. The Committee also most gingerly skirted two major pillars of the existing social and political order: serfdom and autocracy. Both were to remain untouched.

From *Le comte Paul Stroganov* by Grand duc Nicolas Mikhailovitch de Russie (Paris: 1905), Vol. II, Annexe 8; "General Plan for Work with the Emperor on Reform," No. 97, pp. 4-5; "Essay on the System to Be Followed in Reforming the Administration of the Empire," No. 100, pp. 6-11; "On the State of Our Constitution," No. 106, pp. 18-19.

## I. General Plan for Work with the Emperor on the Reform

The first principle to be established is that this reform must be entirely due to His Majesty and that every measure must be taken so that nobody suspects that this work is in progress.

This principle has to be worked out in such a way that there will be no place for doubt in any situation that might arise.

Then it is necessary to picture the goal to be attained, so that one possesses a standard by which to gauge the current business to avoid acting contrary to the principles one wishes to see firmly established.

Then one has to proceed systematically to the work of reform; one will have to begin with the organization of the Committee, the establishment of the principles and plan of work, etc.

To be a good job, the reform must first be a reform of the administration, so that all the parts of the latter are correlated with the security of property and the freedom to do everything that does not harm someone else; in the latter case the law has to foresee the limits beyond which harm to someone else may occur, for everything not prohibited by law is allowed.[1]

Once all this is securely established, one only need discover the barrier that will prevent the arbitrary destruction of this order of things.

This barrier must be found in existing institutions. For to create a new order of things in this respect seems to me very dangerous, and one could create an adequate barrier by giving some luster and privileges to old institutions. The paper of Prince Bezborodko would give the outline of everything one might wish for. . . .

## II. Essay on the System to Be Followed in Reforming the Administration of the Empire (submitted 9 May 1801)

To be secured firmly, the happiness of the people must rest on the elements of domestic prosperity, which in turn depend on the right principles of administration, and not on the empty glory which comes from great influence abroad.

Convinced of this truth, Your Majesty wants to concern Himself with the reform of our government. It is a difficult task, but it is a beautiful one, and the legislator who, after long and arduous labor, has realized some parts of his great design is sure to take with him the benediction of the people, the admiration of the wise, and the title of benefactor of his country.

Your Majesty will not be able to accomplish this honorable task alone; no doubt He will deem it necessary to take collaborators. In what way will these persons collaborate in accomplishing this great enterprise? This is what I propose to discuss, and the following are the principles which, I believe, ought to determine the decisions He will take with respect to this problem.

In order for the reform to entail few of the inconveniences which all too frequently are the consequences of such a transformation, it has to be implemented as gradually as possible. Such a result can be obtained only by evaluating the projected change

---

[1] "A law shall never be retroactive." [This note appears in the original.]

in a way that will make its implementation easy and least likely to experience obstacles.

The basis of this evaluation must be *a sure knowledge of the public's opinion and of the measures likely to prevent any unfavorable prejudice* [from developing].

Knowledge of public opinion can be acquired only by careful and constant observation of the prevailing views concerning the object whose improvement is contemplated. . . .

Any premature rumor can have a bad effect; and the diversity of opinions expressed by prepossessed minds can provide only an erroneous foundation, or at any rate a most uncertain one, for the means of implementation; while tranquillity, which is the result of impenetrable secrecy, will give the government all facility to harmonize its plans with the results of its observations.

One may, therefore postulate the principle that a study of public opinion will yield accurate results only to the extent that secrecy accompanies the government's deliberations. Again, only secrecy will deflect the prejudices which inevitably arise from its absence. . . .

Another predisposition of the human mind which militates in favor of secrecy and which anyone can easily observe is that, forced to submit, man bows much more easily to absolute necessity than to something which seems to leave room for some opposition or struggle.

A law whose preparation has been shrouded in secrecy and which emerges from it without having disturbed the general peace . . . , by demanding all at once equal obedience from all, rather displays the character of necessity, this great law of nature; and any grumbling against it, because it is fruitless, is born and dies almost at the same time; while the law whose aims are revealed in advance, and which disturbs the minds by the uncertainty unavoidably connected with such an imprudent step, arouses an opposition which only a little more discretion might easily have prevented. . . .

Such a long-range and important enterprise demands all possible regularity, so that all its various aspects may be grasped and encompassed. Only the greatest orderliness in the ways in which Your Majesty will deal with this matter will ensure precision in the combinations involved in such a great plan. The method adopted for Your Majesty's work with the Committee must, therefore, be considered one of the constitutive elements in its calculations. . . .

These two fundamental principles having been established, a third, without which nothing good can be done, must be taken into consideration. This is the absolute necessity for the Committee to be in the know of all the operations of the government. . . .

Only by noticing the abuses which practice reveals and by observing carefully their progression may one get to their source, succeed in discerning their principles, and gain knowledge of the most effective ways of preventing, as much as possible, the bad imprint which the instability of things of this world leaves on human institutions. Without this precaution, the work done by this Committee would be only a political dream, quite beautiful in appearance, but whose implementation might have the most disastrous consequences.

Just as radii starting from different points on a circumference converge all at a common center, so all the parts of the administration are mutually interlocked and must converge to the same goal. If, therefore, the movement of the individual parts is not calculated in terms of this general rule, the result can only be an incoherence which will hamper their regular performance.

To avoid this defect, those who are entrusted with the task of renovating the shapeless edifice of our social contract according to correct principles must know the structure of the whole machine; and by constantly keeping in view its movement, they shall be in a better position to see the defects of its wheels and gears. This will enable them to have a better grasp of what improvements are required. . . .

### III. On the State of Our Constitution

To determine anything with respect to this kind of question, one must first agree on the meaning of the word Constitution.

In my opinion, a Constitution is the legal recognition of the rights of a nation and of the manner in which they may be exercised. To insure the validity of these rights, there must exist a guaranty that an alien power will not prevent these rights from being effective. If such a guaranty does not exist, the aim of the exercise of these rights—which consists in preventing any government measure contrary to the true national interest from being taken—would not be attained, and one could then say that there is no Constitution.

The Constitution may, therefore, be divided into three parts: the establishment of rights, the manner of their exercise, and the guaranty.

The first two exist with us, at least in part; but, as we have said, the absence of the third voids completely the other two.

Having said this, I may proceed to a history of our rights.

We have two charters in which a portion of our rights is recorded, the charter of the nobility and the charter of the burghers [*bourgeois*].

The Senate may also be counted among our constitutional institutions (for almost the whole administration of the Empire is entrusted to this body).

The present-day operations of the government must be consonant with its remote aim.

Its remote aim is to establish firmly the happiness of the nation.

This happiness must be real.

What things do then constitute the happiness of men?

The happiness of men consists in the security of their property and in the freedom to do everything with it that does not harm others.

The means for insuring the enjoyment [of what constitutes happiness] are contained in the administrative regulations.

The guardians of these administrative regulations are the fundamental laws of the state, or, in other words, the Constitution.

The Constitution is the law which regulates the method to be observed in the making of administrative rules. Requiring modification and interpretation, these rules must, of necessity, undergo changes in a known, fixed, and invariable manner, in order to close the door to all *arbitrariness* and, consequently, decrease the evil which may result from the difference in talent of those who are at the head of the state.

This is what I mean by Constitution.

Except for it, all other laws are administrative regulations and consequently subject to variation.

The enjoyment of the rights I have defined above entails all the best possible consequences, it is the foundation of all relationships; resting on this security, the human spirit can develop and reach the farthest limits which Nature has set to it; and the enjoyment, as I have said, depends on the goodness of the administrative regulations and on the certainty that they cannot be changed arbitrarily.

The class which in Russia must draw most attention is the peasantry.

This numerous class is composed of individuals who, in large part, are endowed with great intelligence and spirit of enterprise; but, because they are deprived of the enjoyment [of these rights], they are condemned to stagnation, and they cannot let society enjoy the fruits of the labor of which every one of them is capable. They have no fixed status, no property. One can hardly expect much from people in this condition, and the little one sees of their mental efforts is quite astonishing and can but augur well for what they might do if they enjoyed a definite status. But the problem is to provide them with this status without shocks, for otherwise it would be better not to do anything. One must spare the owners and bring them [the peasants] to the goal by a series of ordinances which, without shocks, will produce an improvement in the condition of the peasant and imperceptibly lead to the expected goal. Neither should words imprudently used turn the peasants' heads and thus bring about the most undesirable consequences.

# VI

## Introduction to the Codification of State Laws by M. M. Speransky (1809)

### Introduction

The most comprehensive reform proposal, in fact, a draft for a "constitutional" plan, issued in 1809 from the pen of the State Secretary of Alexander I, Michael M. Speransky (1772-1839). In it, for the first time, we detect an "historicist" approach to the problem of governmental reform on the part of an official of the imperial government. Moreover, to secure the Emperor's assent to a wide-ranging transformation of the order of government to be based on a comprehensive system of principles and theoretical considerations, Speransky adopted an extremely didactic method of exposition. He took pains to explain even the obvious and to make explicit the rationale for every step; as a result, he frequently repeated the same idea in various contexts and in different guises. The document is, therefore, very long and—to the modern reader—quite verbose and redundant. It was, therefore, necessary to be very selective, omitting repetitions in argument and summarizing organizational details.

Speransky followed in the footsteps of Panin, Bezborodko, the authors of the Charter, and the members of the Unofficial Committee in pressing for basic rights guaranteeing security of person and property to the various classes of the population. But, unlike his predecessors, Speransky also provided that the central government should maintain contact with the population of the Empire by means of a hierarchy of narrowly representative *dumas* (councils). He also aimed at introducing clearer chains of command and greater regularity into administrative procedures. Whether these proposals added up to a genuinely constitutional regime for Russia, an opinion held by generations of Russian intellectuals and many historians, the reader may judge for himself.

From *M. M. Speranskii—Proekty i zapiski,*
ed. by S. N. Valk (Moscow-Leningrad: 1961),
pp. 143-221.

Worldly empires have their periods of greatness and of decline, and in each the form of government ought to correspond to the level of the state's [political] civilization. Every time that the form of government falls below or anticipates this level, it is overthrown with more or less violent upheavals. . . .

And thus, time is the first principle and source of all political innovations ("Le plus grand novateur est le temps"—Bacon). No government out of tune with the spirit of its time can withstand its powerful action.

Thus, the first and principal question which must be answered on the threshold of any political transformation is that of its timeliness. . . .

(1) The initiatives [at transformation] under the empresses Anna and Catherine II were, obviously, premature, and therefore they were quite unsuccessful. (2) Within the general course of the progress of human//Original: *political*//reason, our state is in the second period of the feudal system, i.e., in the period of absolutism, and the trend is doubtlessly straight in the direction of freedom. Note: In truth, this movement is straighter with us than it has

been in other states. The reasons are as follows: (1) From the very beginning we have destroyed the right of primogeniture; in other states which have followed the same path this institution has been a big stumbling block. (2) The experiments with transformations that have been carried out around us had, no doubt, a powerful influence on the minds of the majority of individuals concerned [in this country]. (3) In general, in Russia progress is incomparably faster than in other states in similar periods.

. . . Regretfully, one may surely say that at the present time no government measure requiring moral assent and not merely physical submission can have any success. . . . For this there is only one true reason: the present turn of ideas is in complete opposition to the form of government.

Everybody complains of the confusion and chaos of our civil laws. But how can one correct and secure them without solid political laws? . . .

One may conclude with confidence that the present system of government no longer corresponds to the public spirit and that the time has come to change it and to establish a new order of things. . . .

*On the general principle of the transformation:* The general object of the transformation is to set up and base on immutable laws the government which, heretofore, has been autocratic.

Administration cannot be based on law if the sovereign power alone makes the law and executes it. Original: Therefore, one must of necessity admit popular participation in the making of law. Hence the necessity of institutions for drafting and executing the law.

From the tripartite division of government forces stems the tripartite division of these institutions. One of them should act in the making of laws, the other in their execution, and the third in the judiciary. Each institution may be based on a different principle. . . .

Two manners of institutional organization can be noted at first glance: The first consists in clothing autocratic rule into all the external, so to say, appurtenances of legality, leaving the full extent and full force of autocracy untouched in fact. The second manner not only consists in clothing autocracy in external forms, but in limiting it by the instrinsic and essential power of institutions and in establishing a sovereign power[1] based on law not only in words but in deeds. . . .

1. [If the second approach is adopted] the legislative body[2] must be organized in such a way that its statutory purpose may not be fulfilled without the sovereign power, and also so that its opinions are free and express those of the people.

2. The judiciary body must be organized in such a manner that its existence depends on free election, and that only the supervision of judicial procedures and the safeguard of public order belong to the government.

3. The executive power must be entrusted in its entirety to the government; but in the guise of directives for the execution of laws the power of government could not only disfigure the laws, but even destroy them completely, and it should therefore be correlated with the legislative power. . . .

The order of legislation consists of three parts: initiative, consideration, and confirmation. . . .

There can be no doubt, it seems, that legislative initiative must be left completely to the government. The size of the Empire, the variety of its populations, and the level of our civilization require that the government dispose of all the necessary power to act for the good; and this power should be limited only with respect to the above.

If in some cases the source of law is put outside the limits of sovereign power, it may lead to an excessive variety in forms and to a lack of coordination. Time will then often be lost in the legislative assembly on proposals which are untimely and out of place, and, for the sake of the orderly consideration of these proposals in the legislative body, there will have to be established a great number of procedural forms whose safeguard, especially with us, may give rise to excessive complications and difficulties. The government may then be put in the unpleasant situation of

---

[1] *Derzhavnaia vlast'*. In Speransky's vocabulary "sovereign power" meant the power of the autocratic monarch.

[2] In the eighteenth and early nineteenth centuries, and more particularly in Speransky's vocabulary, the term *soslovie* meant not only an estate, but a group of persons with an administrative function.

rejecting or disapproving matters which will have been adopted by the legislative body. . . .

But the following exceptions should be allowed in the foregoing: (1) when a government measure clearly violates the basic law of the state, for example, with regard to personal or political freedom; (2) when the government fails at the set time to submit the accounts required by law. Only in these two cases, and after informing the government, may the legislative body take up the matter for consideration and, on its own initiative, in the manner prescribed by law, institute inquiry proceedings against the minister who has signed the measure, while at the same time requesting the latter's abrogation. . . .

The nature of the executive branch is such as to require of necessity unity [of action]. This truth is unanimously acknowledged by all. Even in the republics most of the executive power is always entrusted to a single individual.

There can be no doubt, therefore, that in Russia all the executive power must belong to the sovereign power. But it has been observed earlier that the manner of execution can depart from the spirit of the law to such an extent that, if the executive branch is set up without any relation to the legislative order, this may result in the law itself becoming the plaything of arbitrary whim. It is necessary, therefore, to have a responsibility whose form may vary, but whose essence remains the same. . . .

//Officials are responsible individually; the signature under an act is always deemed to have been given freely.//

It is proposed that the judges be elected by the persons for whose sake the court is established. In this way the judiciary power remains within the rights of the sovereign power, but the latter has entrusted its [the power of the judiciary] execution to the election by those very persons who could have complained against the sovereign power itself. . . .

Having entrusted to elected persons the essence of the courts, the sovereign power, however, could not also entrust to these same persons the safeguard of the procedure. Judicial procedures constitute an integral part of public law; of necessity they must be uniform. They are so essential to justice that any modification or violation with respect to them frequently changes the very essence of a case. . . . For this reason the safeguard of judicial procedures must rest on the same principle of unity as does the executive power.

According to this concept, the judiciary consists of two institutions: the first, which pertains to the essence of a case, the sovereign power entrusts to the choice of the subjects; and relinquishing, as it were, its responsibility, transfers it to the same source from which derives the legislative power. The second, i.e., the supervision and safeguard of judiciary forms, together with the responsibility appertaining thereto, remains exclusively with the executive order. It follows from this that the action of the sovereign power with respect to the courts should be limited to the sole establishment of that authority which supervises and safeguards judiciary procedures. . . .

If the notion of law is extended to cover all decisions without exception, then everything will become an object for the legislative body; there will be total confusion, and unity of action will disappear with respect to execution.

If, on the contrary, the notion of law is restricted to such an extent that it refers only to the most general statutes, the executive power will have no limits, and under the guise of implementing the laws it will destroy law itself. It is necessary to find the true middle ground and define those traits which differentiate the law from executive measures and various regulations. . . .

In the first place, there must be set up rules for bringing about any changes in the relationship of political forces or in the relationship between private individuals. In the second place, rules [must be established] which merely define the manner of implementing the first without introducing any substantial changes.

To the first group properly belongs the name of law, to the second that of statutes and regulations. The first must be the object of the legislative body's concern, the second belongs to the executive power. . . .

From this it follows that: (1) no law can have legal force if it has not been drafted in the legislative body; (2) statutes and regulations, on the other hand, are within the power of the government, but the latter is responsible to see that they do not violate the law; (3) the government may relinquish this responsibility by submitting the statutes and regulations to the legislative body. . . .

The Russian nation is divided into three classes. The first class, the nobility, consists of the remnants of the old feudal order under which the sovereign power (i.e., the combination of political and civil rights) was divided among illustrious families. In the course of time, the political rights were wrested from them, but their civil rights have been left intact and are hereditarily shared by the families with the sovereign power. The second class—the merchants, burghers, etc.—was formed by transfer from the third and its gradual emancipation.

The third class, the serfs, at first enjoyed some measure of civil rights. They could own property, and they had the right to move from one estate to another. But subsequently, as the political rights were taken from the appanaged lords and annexed by the sovereign power, the civil rights of the third class, as if in compensation to the first, were transferred [from the peasants] to their landlords; and finally, due to various circumstances, but especially because of the system of recruiting for our military forces, the serfs, tied to the land, lost their personal as well as material freedom. . . .

There can be only two sources for all social divisions: civil and political rights.

The first source, civil rights, i.e., the security of person and property, are the primary and intangible possession of any person entering society. It is contrary to human nature to assume that anyone would consent to live in a society in which neither his life nor his property were secured.

There have always been slaves. . . . But from this, one should not conclude that civil slavery is necessary. The makeup of the ancient republics and the customs of the times were the cause of its establishment. On the other hand, we see large and populous states in which this type of slavery has gradually been abolished. There is no reason to believe that it could not be abolished in Russia if active measures were taken to this end. But to be effective, these measures must be gradual.

Civil freedom has two main aspects: personal freedom and material freedom. The essence of the first consists of the following two propositions: (1) No one may be punished without trial. (2) No one need render personal services, except as determined by law, and not by someone's arbitrary decision.//Note: By removing the right to try from the owners, the first proposition gives serfs the right to trial and puts them on a basis of equality before the law with everybody [else]. The second deprives them of the right to give away into [army] service out of turn. Personal freedom is based on these two principles.//

The essence of freedom of the second type, i.e., material freedom, is based on the following propositions: (1) Everyone may freely dispose of his property in conformity with the law; no one may be deprived of property without trial. (2) No one may be compelled to render material services or pay taxes and dues except as established by law or contract, and not by someone's arbitrary decision.//Original: Comparing these two types of civil freedom, one may readily notice that the first, i.e., personal freedom, may be introduced into Russia now and at once. For this, one only has to (i) establish peasant courts and a rural police; (ii) put army recruiting on the private estates on the same footing as in the state villages. But material freedom cannot be introduced in full as long as private serfs have no property. For to give the right to dispose of property when it [property] does not exist is to give an impossible right. From this it follows that, under present conditions, one can only give recognition to this right in general and prepare for its implementation by allowing private serfs to acquire property; until that time, however, one must of necessity be content to ground on law the serfs' obligations vis-à-vis their owners, which will be the main object of the rural statute. From this it follows that the fundamental law may already establish the general principle of equal civil rights, personal and material, for all subjects and, consequently, prohibit any distinction of status in this respect.//

Should both types of civil rights be given to all subjects without any limitations? Two considerations may be set forth:

1. With respect to personal freedom: The law defining personal freedom cannot be the same for all. There are categories of service which require special education and knowledge and which cannot be combined with all kinds of enterprises. Such is service in the higher ranks of the judiciary, the administration, the military. If

one were to permit equal access to service and treat everybody without distinction according to the same rule, then the higher ranks would be filled with individuals not prepared by their education, and one of the most important objects of public education would disappear. . . . Here is the first distinction which must of necessity be allowed in personal civil rights; no one may be deprived of them, but not everyone may enjoy them to the same degree.

2. With respect to material freedom: Property is the foundation of material freedom. The law defining this property should also have its degrees. To all without distinction should belong the right to movable and real property, but not to settled lands, for ownership of settled lands entails relationships of which not everyone is capable. It implies administration, and hence a knowledge of the laws of government, which may not be obtained without special education. . . . From this it follows that ownership of settled real estate may not be enjoyed by all without distinction, and there must be a class to which this right belongs exclusively.

The following general conclusions can be drawn from the above:

### Civil Rights

I. Civil rights, personal and material, are divided into two categories: those common to all Russian subjects and those particular to some estates.

A. Common civil rights: (1) No one may be punished without trial. (2) No one may be compelled to render services at someone's arbitrary command, but only on the basis of the law defining the nature of service according to estates. (3) Anyone may acquire real and movable property and dispose of it in lawful manner; but the acquisition of settled real estate is a right belonging only to specified persons. (4) No one may be compelled to furnish material dues at someone's arbitrary command, but he may be obliged to do so on the basis of law or contract freely entered into.

B. Particular civil rights: (1) to be exempt from the general order of [army] service, but not from the particular services which the law imposes on some estates; (2) the right to acquire settled real estate, but to administer it only according to law.

### Differences in Civil Rights

II. From the differences in civil rights, common and particular, derive the differences among estates, which of necessity must be accepted. . . .

Political rights are another source for division into estates. As indicated above, they consist in participating in the legislative, judiciary, and executive powers of the government. Should political rights belong equally to all Russian subjects? . . .

There can be no doubt that persons owning property should, without distinction, be admitted to participate in political rights. But if individuals without property are also admitted to participate, then, because of their number, the voice and opinion of the latter will no doubt prevail; consequently, all the electoral power of the people will pass into the hands of those very individuals who have the least part in the goodness of these elections and the least ability for correct judgment. On this [consideration] is based the important rule which in all states—even in France in the midst of revolution—restricts the right to vote to those individuals who own property. There is no doubt that we, too, should follow this rule, and therefore provide that no one may participate in elections if he does not own real estate or a specified amount of business capital.

Furthermore, in society there are conditions in which the way of life and education do not warrant the supposition that the persons occupying them have adequate reason or enough ambition to be allowed to make laws. Such is the condition of domestic servants, artisans, laborers, and journeymen, even though they may own capital. . . .

From this survey of the civil and political rights it appears that they all can be divided into three classes: (1) common civil rights belonging to all subjects; (2) particular civil rights which ought to belong only to those who are prepared for them by their way of life and education; (3) political rights belonging to those who own property. From this follows the division into estates: (1) nobility, (2) men of the middle estate, (3) working people. Having thus defined the division into estates, one has to indicate with precision (1) the rights belonging to each estate and its composition, (2) the method of passing from one estate into the other.

### Rights of the Nobility

I. *The rights of the nobility:* (1) The nobility enjoys all the civil rights belonging to all Russian subjects in general. (2) Besides these common rights, the nobility has the particular right of freedom from personal regular [army] service; but [the nobleman] is obliged to serve for at least ten years in a civil or military capacity, as he chooses, but without the right to transfer from one to the other, except in cases specifically defined by law. (3) The nobility has the particular right to acquire settled real estate and to administer it according to law. (4) The nobility has the right to election and representation, but only on the basis of property. (5) All free occupations permitted by law are open to noblemen. They may enter the merchant profession and other callings without losing their estate rights. (6) The nobility is divided into personal and hereditary nobility; personal nobility does not extend beyond one individual. (7) Hereditary nobility is acquired by birthright in conjunction with service. (8) Children of a hereditary nobleman, until they have completed the required number of years of service, enjoy personal nobility. Upon termination of their service, they acquire hereditary nobility by right. (9) Personal nobility—not by birthright—is acquired through service. (10) Children of personal nobles belong to the middle estate. (11) Personal nobility, however, cannot be tranformed into hereditary nobility through service alone. Special merits are required, in recognition of which hereditary nobility is granted and confirmed by special diploma by the Emperor, either in the course of service or upon its completion. (12) Titles of personal nobility make for personal nobility, while hereditary titles give right to hereditary nobility. (13) Preservation of these titles, as well as of the right of nobility, also depends on continuation in service. (14) Hereditary nobility is ended and changed into personal nobility by evasion of service. (15) In general, nobility is forfeited: (a) by judgment of a court, and public punishment; (b) by entrance into the estate of working people.

**Rights of the Middle Estate**

II. *The rights of the middle estate:* (1) The middle estate enjoys the common civil rights but does not have particular ones. (2) The personal services of members of the middle estate are defined by their calling and business on the basis of special legislation. (3) Persons of the middle estate have political rights on the basis of their property. (4) All free occupations are open to [individuals from the middle estate]; they may freely change over from one to another after they have fulfilled the obligations to which they are subjected. (5) They attain personal nobility through service which they enter of their free will, but not before they have fulfilled the services required of them by law by virtue of their previous calling. (6) The middle estate consists of merchants, burghers, artisans, yeomen [*odnodvorets*], and all farmers owning a specified amount of real property.

**Rights of the Working People**

III. *The rights of the working people:* (1) Working people enjoy the common civil rights but no political rights. (2) Passage from their estate into the next is open to all who have acquired a specified amount of real property and fulfilled all the services and paid all the dues of their previous condition. (3) In the class of working people are included all private serfs, artisans and their workers, and domestic servants. . . .

Above all, this division into estates respects [the practice] of gradual progress and the passage from a lower to a higher estate. For this purpose there is established in each estate a link, so to say, connecting it with the next higher. Thus, personal nobility links the first estate to the second. The acquisition of real property links the second with the third; and in this manner individuals who, by virtue of their condition, do not have political rights may wish and hope [to acquire] them by dint of their work and enterprise. . . .

The basic organic laws must define the organization of those institutions through which the state's powers manifest themselves. These institutions are: the Council, the legislative body, the Senate, and the Ministries. . . . Each one of them, combining in the sovereign power and forming the principal government bodies, must extend its authority to the whole Empire and, by means of gradual subdivisions, reach into the lowliest settlements. . . .

//Not only is the Empire divided on the basis of distances, but the subdivisions take into account the number of inhabitants. They also admit of some variety. The Empire is divided into regions [*oblast'*] and provinces [*guberniia*]. The regions encompass areas which by virtue of the character of their population cannot be dealt with on the same uniform basis as the rest of the Empire (Siberia, Caucasus, Astrakhan and Georgia, Orenburg, Don Territory, Novorossiisk). The provinces have one hundred to three hundred thousand souls and are subdivided into two to five districts [*okrug*]; the districts contain several townships [*volost'*] and township towns [*volostnoi gorod*]; big townships may be subdivided into encampments [*stan*].//

### Legislative Order

*First Level*

In every township town or in the main township village an assembly composed of all owners of real property meets every three years under the name of township duma. State villages send one elder from every five hundred to the duma. As its first order of business, the township duma elects a chairman and secretary. In the township duma all voices are equal. No one can delegate his vote *in absentia*. The township duma deals with: (i) election of members of the township administration; (ii) accounts of receipts and disbursement of monies entrusted to the township administration; (iii) election of deputies to the district duma, whose number may not exceed two thirds of all property owners; (iv) drawing up a roster of twenty most distinguished inhabitants of the township, including those who are not in residence; (v) representations to the district duma concerning the public needs of the township. Having dealt with these matters, the duma is dissolved, and its place is taken by the elected administration. The dates and length of the duma's sessions and its rules are to be determined by special law.

### Second Level

Every three years in the district town the deputies of township dumas come together in an assembly called the district duma. The district duma elects a chairman and chief secretary. Votes are equal in the duma. The district duma is concerned with: (i) the election of members of the district council; (ii) the election of members of the district court; (iii) election of deputies to the provincial duma, whose number may not exceed two thirds of the membership of the district duma; (iv) from the lists submitted by the township dumas, drawing up a roster of twenty distinguished inhabitants of the district, those absent not being excluded from the roster; (v) an account by the preceding administration of the monies collected for public expenditures; (vi) representations to the district duma of public needs based on an examination of the representations made by the township duma. For the examination of accounts and the representations of needs the duma sets up two commissions from its own members. Having taken care of these matters, the duma is dissolved. The date and duration of the sessions and their procedures are fixed by special law.

### Third Level

Every three years in the provincial capital the deputies from the district dumas meet in an assembly called the provincial duma. Upon assembling, the provincial duma first elects a president and secretary. All members have an equal voice in the provincial duma, and those absent may not delegate their votes. The provincial duma deals with: (i) the election of members to the provincial council; (ii) the election of members of the provincial court; (iii) election of members to the State Duma from the two estates enjoying political rights—their number is set by law for each province; (iv) drawing up a roster of twenty most distinguished inhabitants of the province, not excluding those absent; (v) accounts of the administration of monies collected for public expenditures; (vi) representation on public needs on the basis of the representations of the district dumas. For the examination of accounts and the representations of needs the duma appoints two commissions from its [own] membership.

Having taken care of these matters, the president forwards to the Council of State under signature of all members of the assembly the following: (I) for the Chancellor of Justice, a list of all those elected to township administration and to district and provincial courts; (II) for the Chancellor of the State Duma, lists of: (a) members elected to district and provincial councils, (b) members elected to the legislative body, (c) most distinguished inhabitants of the province, (d) representations on the province's needs. With this the task of the provincial duma is completed, and its place is taken by the provincial council. . . .

### Fourth Level

The deputies elected by the provincial duma constitute a legislative body called the State Duma. The State Duma is an institution equal to the Senate and the Ministry. Under provision of the fundamental law and without special convocation, the State Duma sits every year in September. The length of its session depends on the amount of business submitted. The action of the State Duma may be stopped by: (1) adjournment to the following year; (2) dismissal of all its members. Adjournment takes place by virtue of an act of the sovereign power taken in the Council of State. Dismissal takes place by virtue of a similar act which, however, also lists the new members [chosen among those] nominated at the last election of provincial dumas.

Except for a general dismissal, members of the State Duma may not relinquish their seat, except through death, decision of the Supreme Court, or through appointment to the Council, the Senate, or the Ministry. In the latter cases, their place is immediately taken by a candidate from the list drawn up at the last election. The president of the State Duma is elected from its members and is confirmed by the sovereign power. A special official, under the name of Secretary of the State Duma, is appointed to assist him. At its first meeting, the State Duma organizes the following legislative commissions: (1) for state laws, (2) for civil laws, (3) for statutes and regulations, (4) for ministerial accounts or accounts of responsibility, (5) for the representation of needs of the state, (6) for finances. Each commission has its chairman and secretary elected by the Duma. Matters are submitted to the State Duma in the name of the sovereign power by one of the Ministers or members of the Council of State. Excepted from this rule are: (1) representations on state needs, (2) representations on shirking of responsibility, (3) representations concerning measures violating the fundamental laws of the state. In these three cases, established procedure having been respected, the initiative may be taken by members of the Duma. Incidentally, the procedures of the Duma's action and discussion and decision are defined in detail in the fundamental laws.

### The Judiciary

//Township courts are similar to justices of the peace.// . . . The law defines some types of cases, particularly original ones, which the chief township judge may decide only after having invited [the participation] of //Note: two; original: three// deputies from the township council who act as jurymen, while the judge is their president [*directeur de jury*]. //Note: Both deputies, or at least one, are selected from the estate to which the accused belongs. If there are no such jurors available, the accused is remanded to the district court.// . . . //The district court consists of two divisions: criminal and civil. The president of each is selected from the twenty most distinguished inhabitants of the district. The law defines the cases to be tried with jury on the model of the township court. The provincial courts are organized on a basis similar to the district courts. The Senate is the highest court of the Empire; it has four departments (two civil and two criminal, one of each in each capital). The decisions of the Senate are published. Special cases involving high dignitaries are tried by a Supreme Criminal Court organized within the Senate.//

### The Executive

//Four levels: state (ministry), provincial, district, and township.//
//The Ministry based on the law of 1802 has three drawbacks:

lack of responsibility, bad distribution of competencies, lack of precise rules of procedure. Propose to have seven ministries: external affairs, military, navy, interior, finances, police, justice. Detailed list of the state's functions in the economic life of the country as they are distributed among the ministries of the interior, the police, and finances. The business of the provincial administration is organized along the same lines as the ministries. The provincial government consists of the provincial administration and the Chamber of the Treasury. The provincial government is subdivided into the following bureaus: police, industry, treasury; and every bureau has as many departments as there are problem areas. Each bureau has one administrator and operates on the basis of its own statute and regulations. In important cases the bureaus gather in a general assembly under the chairmanship of the governor. The governor supervises all areas of administration, and the Ministers transmit their orders through him. He is responsible to the ministry, and the administrators are responsible to him. In every bureau there are some matters that may not be decided without his approval. Every provincial government has a council of deputies of all estates owning real property in the province. The Council meets once a year at a set time. The governor accounts for expenditures and receipts of dues and submits the budget. The Council makes its comments on the accounts.//

//The district administration is organized on a basis similar to the provincial one, only on a smaller scale. The township administration follows a similar pattern, but on a smaller and more simplified scale.//

//The fundamental laws will define the organization of the Council of State, its nature, and the form of its procedure.//

I. In the order of state institutions the Council is the body [*soslovie*] in which the principal actions of the legislative, judiciary, and executive are unified, and through it they ascend to the sovereign power or are handed down from it.

II. For this reason the preliminary drafts of all laws, statutes, and regulations are submitted to and examined in the Council of State; and by act of the sovereign power they are then forwarded for implementation.

III. No law, statute, or regulation may issue from the Council of State and be implemented without the sovereign power's confirmation.

IV. The Council is composed of persons called to it by the Sovereign's confidence.

V. Members of the Council may have offices in the judiciary and executive branches.

VI. Ministers are members of the Council *ex officio.*

VII. The Emperor or a member personally appointed by Him presides over the Council.

VIII. Appointment to the presidency of the Council is renewed every year at the discretion of the Sovereign.

IX. The Council is divided into the following departments: (1) laws, (2) military affairs, (3) civil and religious affairs, (4) state economy.

X. Every department has a specified number of members, one of whom is the chairman.

XI. Members of all the departments constitute the general assembly of the Council.

XII. Members not appointed to specific departments attend the general assemblies.

XIII. The assignments to departments and chairmanships are renewed every half year at the Sovereign's discretion.

XIV. Departments and general assemblies meet on set days, but in consideration of pending business they may be called at any time by imperial command.

XV. All the decisions issuing from the Council upon approval by the Sovereign receive the following form: (1) Statutes, resolutions, and their amendments are in the form of manifestos beginning [with the following words]: "Having heard the opinion of the Council, We order or rule, etc." (2) Clarification of statutes and regulations which do not innovate but which precisely define the meaning of those issued previously are in the form of reports which are approved [by the Sovereign] with the formula: "So be it."

//Last three pages deal with the internal organization of the departments and the Council.//

# IIV

# N. N. Novosil'tsev:
# Constitutional Charter of
# the Russian Empire (1818-1820)

————◆————

## Introduction

After 1815, having become more than ever aware of the multinational character of the Empire by the incorporation of Finland as an autonomous unit and the granting of a separate constitution to the "Congress Kingdom" of Poland, the Russian government developed interest in schemes of reform involving a deconcentration of administrative authority. Such was, for instance, Balashov's plan (1818) of combining several provinces [*guberniia*] into a single governor-generalship, with wide scope of administrative responsibility and authority entrusted to the governor-general. Novosil'tsev's proposal for a constitutional charter—drafted between 1818 and 1820 —belongs in this same context.

The charter is remarkable for the fact that Novosil'tsev bases his proposals much along the lines of what Speransky had advocated or implemented in 1809-12 and combines them with elements quite obviously suggested by Polish practice. It is one of the few instances in Russian administrative history of a proposal along genuinely federal lines. In fact, by giving every vicegerency virtual autonomy in all matters of local concern and significance, it comes close to conceiving the Russian state as the sum total of these vicegerencies, rather than as an entity in itself.

There was no attempt made to implement the charter, and it lay buried in the papers of Novosil'tsev until the Polish revolutionaries published it in 1831.

From *Russkii Arkhiv*, 43rd year (Moscow: 1905), tome III, pp. 104-28.

1. The Russian state, with all the possessions (by whatever name) annexed to it, is divided (as per attached roster) into large regions called vicegerencies [*namestnichestvo*].

2. Each vicegerency contains a specified number of provinces [*guberniia*], depending on population, distances, and area, and taking into consideration the mores, customs, and special or local laws which bind the inhabitants together. . . .

9. The crown of the Russian imperial throne is hereditary; it is transmitted in accordance with the order established by our late Father, Emperor Paul.

10. The principles of sovereign power[1] and the form of its action are defined by the present Constitutional Charter, granted by Us to Our beloved subjects in perpetuity.

11. The sovereign power is indivisible; it is concentrated in the person of the Monarch.

12. The Sovereign is the sole source of all authority in the Empire: civil, political, legislative, and military. He administers the executive branch in all its manifestations. All authorities— executive, administrative, and judiciary—are appointed by him alone.

13. But in [the exercise of] his legislative power, the Monarch is assisted by the State Diet [*seim*] to be mentioned below, on the basis of the Constitutional Charter and special statutes.

---

[1] Sovereign power (*derzhavnaia vlast'*) means here, as it did in Speransky's Plan, the power of the autocratic monarch; cf. G. Vernadsky, *La Charte Constitutionnelle de l'Empire russe de l'an 1820* (Paris: 1933), p. 132.

14. The person of the Monarch is sacred and inviolable.

15. The Monarch is the supreme head of the general administration of the Empire. He takes care of the internal and external security of the state. He watches over his [own] rights and possessions. . . .

24. The Monarch disposes of the revenue of the state in accordance with the particular budgets of the vicegerencies and the general budget of the state approved by him. . . .

26. In order to define the legislative action of the Monarch, the general legal foundations of the Empire are divided into three categories: (1) laws [zakon]; (2) acts and statutes [ustav, uchrezhdenie]; (3) decrees [ukaz], orders [povelenie], rescripts [reskript], and regulations [postanovlenie].

27. By "laws" are to be understood all legislative decisions which are based on inviolable principles and which may be abrogated or amended only if their principles are preserved inviolate, and even then only either if experience has shown the necessity of change or if required by weighty and compelling considerations.

28. By "acts" and "statutes" should be understood all the measures required by circumstances for the defense of the state and the inviolability of its borders, for the organization of internal administration, and, finally, for measures pertaining to government service and the increase in general and individual welfare.

29. Finally, under the terms "decrees," "orders," "rescripts," and "regulations" are subsumed all orders given in particular and special circumstances that may arise in various areas of state administration, or everything that pertains to an office, a military or civil official, or a private person, and which by its nature is subject to changes depending on need.

30. Laws are divided into general laws of the state and particular laws. The general laws constitute the law which is applied in all cases when local laws are inadequate.

31. General laws are issued by the Monarch with the assistance of the General Diet of the State, as will be shown below.

32. Particular or local laws are given by the Monarch with the assistance of the Diets of the vicegerencies.

33. The power to issue statutes, acts, decrees, rescripts, and regulations belongs exclusively to the Monarch. He may delegate

this power, in part or in full, to persons or institutions of his choosing. . . .

35. The Council of State, under the presidency of the Monarch, consists of ministers [who are] members of the Council, State Referendaries or State Secretaries, and persons to whom His Imperial Majesty will deem advisable to give membership in it.

36. The Council of State is divided into a General Assembly of the Council and the Governing Council or Committee of Ministers.

37. The Governing Council, under the chairmanship of the Monarch, is composed of ministers [who are] heads of administrations, and other persons designated at the Monarch's pleasure.

38. The members of the Governing Council have an advisory voice. The Monarch alone decides. His Majesty may delegate this right, in full or in part, to his lieutenant in the Governing Council or to whomever he designates. The latter are obliged to make decisions in Council according to the statutory rules and laws of the state.

39. The Governing Council or Committee of Ministers may annul regulations issued by vicegerents [sitting] in council of vicegerencies if they are contrary to the laws, statutes, decrees, orders, and rescripts given to the vicegerent. Under similar circumstances, the Governing Council may also abrogate the decisions and orders of lower administrative institutions, in case intermediate authorities have failed to do so. . . .

42. //Competence of the General Assembly of the Council of State is defined by the act of 1809.// . . .

45. Execution of the laws is entrusted on the basis of the general statute of the Ministries of 25 June 1811 to the following ministries and chief administrations [follows list]. . . .

47. In every region organized as a vicegerency there will be appointed a vicegerent [*Namestnik*] and there will be established a Council of the Vicegerency, both to reside in a specified locality.

48. Together with the Council, and on the basis of prescribed procedure, the vicegerent takes care of the welfare of the provinces entrusted to him and supervises the precise execution of the laws and orders of higher authorities in all fields of administration.

49. The Council is under the chairmanship of the vicegerent

and is divided into a Governing Council and a General Assembly.

50. The Governing Council is composed of the vicegerent, a specified number of members, and all other persons called to it by command of the Sovereign. There is in addition an executive secretary with full rights of membership. . . .

52. Members of the Council have an advisory voice. The vicegerent decides. He must decide in council in accordance with the statutory rules of the state, the laws, and the powers given to him.

53. Every member of the Council who is in charge of a branch of administration must countersign all the vicegerent's decisions and orders pertaining to his branch. If he disagrees with the [vicegerent's] decision, he may enter his opinion in the minutes; he is then relieved from all responsibility [with respect to it]. . . .

58. The General Assembly of the Council of the vicegerency consists of the persons mentioned in article 50 above and of members elected by the various provinces of the vicegerency and approved by His Majesty the Emperor on recommendation of the Committee of Ministers.

59. The statutory meetings of the General Assembly of the Council of the vicegerency occur at the time of the election and convocation of the Diets. At other times it meets only at the Monarch's command or if summoned by the vicegerent. The General Assembly discusses in general all matters pertaining to the administration of the vicegerency, as well as those submitted by order of His Majesty the Emperor or at the suggestion of the Committee of Ministers and the vicegerent. In particular, it is concerned with the apportionment and collection of taxes, the establishment of local dues, economizing on state expenditures, and increasing the state's revenue within the limits of the vicegerency, and with the expansion of agriculture, industry, trade, etc. . . .

63. The law proclaims as an inviolable principle the separation of administrative and judiciary functions; their respective actions, being incompatible, may never, under any circumstances, be combined. . . .

78. The Orthodox Greek-Russian faith shall always be the dominant faith of the Empire, the Emperor, and the whole imperial family. It will always enjoy the special solicitude of the government, without the other creeds being oppressed, however. Membership in

different Christian denominations does not entail any distinctions in civil and political rights. . . .

80. The law gives equal protection to all citizens without any distinction.

81. The fundamental Russian law, "No one is to be punished without trial," and the rule sanctified by the Statute on the Provinces [1775] (article 401), "No one may be deprived of his freedom and held in prison without being informed of his crime and without a statement being taken from him within three days after arrest," [2] are extended to all the inhabitants in the following manner:

82. No one may be arrested, accused, deprived of his freedom except in cases provided by law and in accordance with prescribed procedures.

83-88. //Further technical details on right to bail, *ex post facto* legislation.//

89. Freedom of the press is guaranteed. The law sets forth the rules for controlling abuses. . . .

91. From now on and forever, the Russian people shall have a popular representation. It shall consist of a State Diet (State Duma) composed of the Monarch and two chambers. The first, by the name of Upper Chamber, consists of the Senate; the second, by the name of Chamber of Ambassadors, is composed of local ambassadors and deputies of municipalities of district towns. . . .

97. All property, whether on the surface of the soil or hidden in the bowels of the earth, whatever its nature and whoever its owner, is acknowledged to be sacred and inviolate. No authority may infringe on it under any pretext whatever. Whoever infringes on someone else's property is tried and punished as if he had violated the public peace.

98. The government, however, has the right to demand of a private person the sacrifice of his property in return for advance

---

[2] This is in fact a paraphrase. The pertinent part of article 401 of the Statute on the Provinces (7 November 1775, PSZ, No. 14392) reads: "Should someone petition the Court in Equity to the effect that he has been kept in prison for more than three days, and that in the course of these three days he was not informed of the reason why he is kept in prison or if in these three days he has not been interrogated, the Court in Equity shall order. . . ."

and just compensation. The law sets forth the particular cases in which this right may be invoked and the rules which govern it. . . .

100. The State Diet (State Duma) is divided into particular diets [*duma*] of the vicegerencies, called every three years, and a General State Duma or Diet, called every five years. . . .

102. The diets of vicegerencies consist of the Monarch and two chambers. The first, called the Upper Chamber, consists of one department of the Senate having its sessions in the capital of the vicegerency. The second, named Chamber of Ambassadors, is composed of two thirds of the ambassadors and deputies elected within the boundaries of the vicegerency and confirmed by the Monarch.

103. The diets of vicegerencies consider general law projects in all the cases the Monarch deems it advisable to submit to them through the Council of State. Primarily, they consider all projects of particular laws appertaining to the respective vicegerency that are submitted to them by imperial command through the Sovereign Council of the vicegerency. Furthermore, if communicated to them in the name of the Monarch, they consider measures to increase, decrease, or equalize all dues, taxes, or obligations; they discuss the burgets of the vicegerency; in short, they take up everything the Monarch orders submitted to them for consideration.

104. . . . Every diet of a vicegerency examines the instructions [*nakaz*] given to the ambassadors and deputies by their electors and containing the latter's remarks, statements, and petitions on everything regarding their interests. //An extract of these instructions is submitted to the Emperor through the Council of State.// . . .

109. Members of the Council [of the vicegerency] have the right to attend debates and take the floor in both chambers [of the diet]. But those who are not senators, ambassadors, or deputies from the land [*zemskii posol*] have no vote. . . .

112. At the time of the diet's adjournment the Chambers of ambassadors from the land and deputies of the diet in every vicegerency proceed to the election of ambassadors and deputies who will constitute the second chamber of the General State Diet. They elect from their own ranks. The number to be elected must equal one quarter of the ambassadors and deputies present. . . .

114. The General State Diet is composed of the Monarch and two chambers. The first, called the Upper Chamber, consists of the department of the Senate sitting in one of the two capitals, with the addition—only for the duration of the Diet and upon appointment by the Monarch—of a specified number of senators from two [other?] departments of the Senate. The second chamber, called Chamber of Ambassadors from the land, is composed of members appointed by the Monarch from the ambassadors and deputies elected in every vicegerency by the Chamber of Ambassadors and numbering one half of those so elected.

115. When they are communicated to it in the name of the Monarch through the Council of State, the General State Diet considers all projects of civil, criminal, and administrative laws pertaining to the whole Empire //and has tasks similar to those enumerated in article 103, only for the whole Empire.// . . .

117. Law projects drafted in the Council of State are submitted, at the Monarch's direction, to the General State Diet by members of the Council. . . .

126. The right to call, dissolve, adjourn, and extend the diets, both in ordinary and extraordinary session, belongs to the Monarch alone. The sessions of the diets last thirty days.

127. The diets may consider only those subjects which are within their competence or specified in the letters of convocation.

128. For the duration of the diets' sessions, no member may be arrested or tried in criminal court without informing the chamber to which he belongs.

129. At his discretion the Monarch may submit projects first to the Senate or to the Chamber of Ambassadors. Excluded from this rule are the financial projects, which must first be submitted to the Chamber of Ambassadors from the land.

130. Projects submitted to the Diet by imperial command are considered to have been neither approved nor confirmed by the Monarch; hence, the Diet is at full liberty to express its opinion.

131. Both chambers hold their discussions publicly, i.e., in the presence of outsiders who are not debarred. At the suggestion of one tenth of the members present, however, they may go into executive session. . . .

133. A project adopted by one chamber may not be modified by the other. It simply must be either accepted or rejected.

134. A project adopted by both chambers is submitted to the Monarch for confirmation.

135. If the Monarch confirms the project, it receives force of law and is published according to established procedure. If the Monarch does not deign to confirm it, the project is annulled.

136. The Senate consists of the Grand Dukes of the imperial family and of all persons who, having fulfilled the appropriate requirements, are elevated to the rank of senator by the Monarch. A senator retains his title to his death.

137. The number of senators is set by the Monarch. It must not be in excess of one quarter of the number of deputies and ambassadors from the land of the whole state.

138. The Senate is divided into several departments, one of which holds its sessions in St. Petersburg and another in Moscow. In addition, one department is appointed for every vicegerency and holds its sessions in the main residence of the latter's administration.

139. Only those may be elevated to the dignity of senator who are at least thirty-five years of age, have had the required experience in lower ranks, have filled with distinction civil and military offices, and have a yearly income of at least one thousand silver rubles from real estate belonging to them in proper. . . .

149-150. //One half of the membership of the Chambers of Ambassadors of the diets in vicegerencies is replaced at every new session of the diet. . . . Members may be re-elected.// . . .

153. One half of the membership of the General State Diet is renewed at every session. . . . Members may be re-elected. . . .

155. To be elected to the Chamber of Ambassadors, [a candidate] must be at least thirty years old, enjoy the rights of citizenship, and pay no less than the specified amount of real estate and other taxes set for each vicegerency, depending on local conditions and population.

156. No civil or military official may be elected to membership in the Chamber of Ambassadors without prior permission from his superiors.

157. If an ambassador or deputy who, prior to his election, did not hold a position on government salary should accept such a position after his election, he must be replaced by a new member. . . .

159. The noblemen in every district who personally own real estate form an assembly of the nobility at which they elect three ambassadors from the land. . . .

161. No nobleman may have a voice in the assembly of the nobility unless he is entered on the roster of the nobility of his district, enjoys the rights of a citizen, has attained the age of twenty-five, and owns real property. . . .

163. //Assemblies of the nobility [*dietins*] may draft instructions [*nakaz*] setting forth their needs, complaints, and suggestions for the welfare of the inhabitants of the district.// . . .

166. [The following] may participate in the elections of deputies from municipalities of district towns [*okruzhnoe gradskoe obshchestvo*]: (a) actual inhabitants of the town who own in it houses or other buildings, a plot, or land, as well as inhabitants from the nobility living outside the town (but within its district) and owning a house or other real estate in that district; (b) all those who are known as "distinguished burghers," [*imenityi grazhdanin*] such as: scholars possessing university or academic diplomas, sculptors and painters, bankers, capitalists, and shipowners; (c) merchants of the first two guilds; (d) master craftsmen.

167. Jews, even those who are enrolled in guilds and own real estate, may not participate in the assemblies of the municipality. . . .

175. Courts and persons holding the title of judge act according to the law and are independent of any authority in the exercise of their functions. . . .

190. Subsequent decrees will define the provinces and regions that are to be combined into vicegerencies and are to enjoy the political rights inherent in popular representations.

191. All previous laws and statutes contrary to this Charter are abrogated.

We grant this Constitutional Charter in good conscience, convinced that the basic statutes listed above correspond to Our paternal wish to give a firm foundation to the prosperity and peace of Our beloved and loyal subjects, to secure the inviolability of their persons and property, and to safeguard the (inalienability) of their civil and political rights. While preserving the right to make additions, We acknowledge it to be—for Ourselves and for Our heirs— the basic and constitutional law of Our state. We command all government authorities to cooperate in bringing about its implementation.

# VIII

## Memorandum of
## State Secretary Valuev
## (13 April 1863)

### Introduction

The reforms initiated in the early years of the reign of Alexander
II put the relations between Russia's "society" and government
into a new perspective. The emancipation of the serfs had been
carried out with the help of representatives of the nobility, who
played a role both in its preparation (provincial commissions) and
in its implementation ("justices of the peace"). Quite clearly, Russian public opinion expected the collaboration between the government and the country's social, economic, and cultural leadership to
be continued and expanded.

But Russia remained a country governed by the Autocrat, assisted by a narrow-minded and restrictive bureaucracy. Awareness
of this situation and uncertainty with respect to the future of the
transformations that had been initiated made public opinion rest-
less. Revolutionary propaganda and radical ideologies heightened
the tension. Well aware of this situation, some highly placed government officials believed it imperative to stop the corroding effect
of this discontent and, in order to preserve the government's au-

thority, to re-establish communications between government and society. Count Petr Aleksandrovich Valuev (1815-90), the Minister of the Interior, put forth an ingenious scheme by which a select group of elected representatives would be called upon to lend the weight of their opinions and knowledge to the deliberations of the Council of State.

From " 'Constitutional' Projects of the Reign of Alexander II," by K. L. Berman'skii in *Vestnik Prava*, XXXV (November, 1905), pp. 225-33.

//In an introduction, Valuev discusses the impact of the Polish revolt of 1863 as evidence of the Russian government's failure and as a war danger.//

For two years the patriotic sentiments of the Russians kept silent. Neither the rebellions of the Poles, nor the slanders of foreigners, nor the lie-filled misrepresentations of our chronicles could shatter this silence. Now it has ceased. The long sleep has been disturbed. The sound of the voice which Your Imperial Majesty's loyal servants have for long and with impatience tried to detect has resounded at long last; and not only does it resound in various corners of Russia, but from everywhere it surges up to the throne of Your Majesty. Wherever the feelings to which these voices bear witness, there lie the path of unity, the foundation of power, the source of strength, and with it the pledge of victory.

The awakening of these feelings is remarkable. It is caused not only by profound loyalty to Your Majesty, or out of a feeling of hurt national dignity, or solely by a concern for the preservation of the state's integrity. The anxious and depressing thought that the rapid pace of events might force Your Majesty to grant to Poland such advantages and privileges which the core areas of Russia would not enjoy have contributed to arouse the upper classes of the Russian people to the full sense of their true loyalty and patriotic duty. This thought comes through in the addresses presented to Your Majesty; but it is heard even louder in the general talk of the masses and the most loyal organs of our press. This is the reason that this time patriotic sentiments are registered more slowly in those parts of the Empire which are not inhabited by the Russian nation, for example, the Baltic provinces. Along with expressions of genuine devotion, profound obedience, and unquestioned readiness to every sacrifice, there also rises to Your Majesty's throne the semi-public entreaties to show confidence in your people, to recognize its capacity to justify this confidence, and to grant it the opportunity of proving that it is worthy of it.

Most gracious Sovereign, grant your beloved and loyal Russia political precedence over rebellious Poland! Allow Russia a step ahead of Poland on the path of progress of government institutions. You will then gather more solidly around you all your loyal subjects. You will then truly be, in the words of the nobility of Moscow, "more powerful than Your Predecessors." You will then definitely secure for Russia the Western patrimony that has been returned to her, washed by the blood of generations. You will at last compel the Western provinces to turn their face to Moscow and their back on Warsaw. Then will the Western question be settled forever and Poland's cause forever lost.[1]

I have taken the liberty of saying that we fear war because in recent times we have felt weak internally. We must look into the causes of this weakness. The financial sores of previous years have not yet healed; the system of transportation has not yet been organized; the great and necessary transformations undertaken by Your Majesty have not been brought to their conclusion; the lack of direction in the activities of various government departments has not yet been eliminated; all the bonds of the country's former system have been weakened while new ones have not yet found firm ground; economic interests are suffering; the minds are in ferment; and meanwhile, taking advantage of the circumstances, revolutionary propaganda endeavors to undermine the very foundations of civil order. But I make bold to believe that all of this is not the main reason for the weakness which we have experienced up to now. For as long as the masses' [peoples'] loyal devotion to Your Majesty and strong love of country have not weakened and have

---

[1] Valuev means the total absorption and russification of the formerly Lithuanian and Polish Western provinces of Russia.

kept their former strength among the overwhelming majority of the upper classes, there are in these very sentiments firm support and an inexhaustible source of strength. The main danger has been the fact that in recent times the practical application of these feelings to various domains of civic life seemed to have been paralyzed by the influence of unfavorable circumstances and various, mostly confused, aspirations and expectations of a transformation in the character of our way of life. Of course, there has been no consensus of opinion concerning the particular aspects and details of this transformation, but there has been almost complete unanimity on its necessity. It seems that a distinction is beginning to be made between the Sovereign Person of Your Majesty and Your government. Everybody is devoted to You personally, but apparently almost nobody quite fully agrees with the system of government decisions. Even the great reforms of the judiciary, for example, have been judged one-sidedly or seen as a pledge for other and more substantial transformations. One idea, apparently, has taken hold of all minds. It has manifested itself in various ways and has taken on various names, at times in resolutions of assemblies of estates, at others in printed works; at times [it has appeared] under guise of "self-government" or "decentralization," at others in a systematic contrast drawn between the government and "society" or the "people"; or again in the form of a doctrine about the *"zemstvo"* [2] and panegyrics of the *Zemskii Sobor* [3] of old. But essentially, it has always been the same idea. Namely, that in all European countries various estates are given some degree of participation in the business of legislation or general administration of the state; and if this is so everywhere, then it should also be the case with us. The establishment of the principles of such a participation is considered a sign of political maturity. Constantly stimulated in a tremendous

---

[2] The reference is to the hope of using the *zemstvo* organization for the gradual development of a constitutional order in Russia; see G. Fischer, *Russian Liberalism* (Cambridge, Mass.: Harvard University Press, 1958).

[3] The panegyrics of the *Zemskii Sobor* (a kind of Estates-General in Muscovite Russia in the sixteenth and seventeenth centuries) were sung by the Slavophiles who saw in this old estate assembly a means for establishing close contact between the people (peasantry) and the Tsar and his government.

number of Russian travelers by what they see abroad and in an even greater number of Russian readers both by the Russian press and by what is printed in all known languages, this notion cannot fail to have a strong, daily increasing influence. The revolutionary agitators cleverly take advantage of this influence; they carry away many [people] and lead them quite far, mainly because these people are not permitted to move toward the goal they themselves would like to reach. Fortunately, as understood and striven for by the vast majority, this goal does not lie outside the bounds of a loyal subject's duties. The notion of participating to some extent in matters of legislation and general state administration does not imply an encroachment on the sovereign rights of the Autocratic power of Your Majesty. The striving for this participation is an expression of the desire to draw nearer to Your Majesty's Throne, to take a place in those institutions through which Your Sovereign will is made known, to bring to you directly the pledge of obedience and civic effort of loyal subjects. These pleas have been made before, and they will doubtlessly be repeated in the future. . . . It will be difficult always to reject such pleas. If it is difficult to reject them definitively, is it not better to forestall them? With this in mind, there has already been suggested for Your Majesty's consideration the proposal to invite a certain number of representatives from the estates of the nobility and of the burghers [*gorodskoe soslovie*], as well as a few members of the higher Orthodox clergy in a consultative capacity in discussions of matters pertaining to it.

At the present time, circumstances again point with renewed force to the usefulness of such a measure. On the one hand, these are the patriotic sentiments which have been awakened after a long sleep and are particularly receptive to it [measure], while at the same time they need its [measure] support to reach their full development in the face of forthcoming trials. Your Majesty's loyal subjects are already drawing closer around You; any Sovereign favor, any sign of the Monarch's trust will be received with redoubled and genuine gratitude. On the other hand, with the introduction of the [administrative] *zemstvo* institutions there will be a need to counteract those aspirations to provincial separatism which have already manifested themselves in some parts of the Empire. This may be brought about with desired success only by a central institution which would provide (in the persons of their representatives) for a confrontation between the interests of some localities and those of other localities, and itself personify the unity of the state and the safeguard of its integrity.

But since the first proposal to invite to the Council of State representatives of the estates, circumstances have changed somewhat. The common striving for participation in governmental affairs that was mentioned earlier has manifested itself with greater force. After the recent elections in St. Petersburg and the memorandum of Platonov[4] it has become impossible to limit oneself to the number of representatives and the manner of their convocation that had been under consideration originally. To preserve consistency in the general order of the transformation undertaken under Your Majesty's directive, it seems to be necessary to tie in the new organization of the Council of State with that of the new *zemstvo* institutions. From this follows that the representatives of the land [*zemstvo*] who are to be invited to the Council of State should be elected by local *zemstvo* institutions. Further, it follows that the representatives of those parts of the Empire to which the *zemstvo* institutions have not been extended—for example, Siberia, the Caucasus region, the Baltic provinces—should also be nominated by election. In this connection the question arises whether one should admit special deputies elected by the assemblies of the nobility, as long as the latter maintain their separate existence; although it is doubtful that these special, elected representatives are necessary. Finally, there arises another question with respect to the great number of persons who might be called upon to participate in the work of the Council: should a single assembly of all members be set up, or should it be divided into two; and in the latter case, what principle of division should be adopted? The details and even the essential particulars of such an important matter cannot, of course,

---

[4] Valuev means the election of a marshal of the nobility in the Province of St. Petersburg. Platonov, the marshal of the nobility of Tsarskoe Selo, developed a resolution expressing the desirability of introducing a system of popular representation in the Empire; his resolution was defeated by the Assembly of the Nobility of the Province of St. Petersburg, but the very fact of its introduction created a deep impression in government circles.

be considered and decided at once in the short time that Your Majesty has given me to submit the present considerations.[5] But if Your Majesty should deign to approve their basic idea and definitely consent to its implementation, and if Your Majesty also deems it convenient and useful to make it public on the seventeenth of this month, then it behooves [me] at least to set forth the basic principles of the proposed measure and to decide the separate question of the way in which Your Majesty's sovereign decision is to be announced.

In my humble opinion, the following could serve as basic principles for the participation, within certain limits, of representatives of various estates in matters of the general government of the state:

1. The participation in question must be only consultative.

2. The assembly of representatives should be affiliated with the Council of State, because the latter, too, has only a consultative role in settling matters within its jurisdiction.

3. Estate or *zemstvo* representatives participate in legislative affairs and extend their participation to major questions of state economy, such as the examination of the state budget and the levying of new taxes.

4. Representatives of *zemstvos* or estates are called from all parts of the Empire except the Kingdom of Poland and the Grand Duchy of Finland.

5. In those parts of the Empire where *zemstvo* institutions will be introduced, the representatives are elected by local *zemstvo* assemblies. For other regions there will be provided special electoral rules.

6. The calling of representatives to the Council of State will not take place before the introduction of the new administrative *zemstvo* institutions.

7. The number of representatives should be as limited as possible. There is no need for separate representatives from the cities. In determining the number for each region of the Empire (about two to four for each province), a ratio can be set for representatives from country districts and from towns.

---

[5] Valuev was asked to present a draft proposal of reform by April 17, 1863.

8. Exceptions may be allowed for the capitals and for the most important commercial centers or provincial capitals, such as Odessa, Riga, Kiev.

9. The representatives receive no monetary compensation from the Treasury.

10. Their participation in the business of the Council of State is limited to a specified period every year. Accordingly, the business of the Council is divided into two categories: matters to be discussed only with the deputies participating, and matters which can be decided without them or with the participation of only some deputies.

11. The order of business will be established in such manner as to reserve the necessary share of influence to the appointed members of the Council, with respect both to procedure and to decisions to be reached. The procedures by which affairs and decisions of the Council of State are presented for the sovereign command and confirmation of Your Majesty should be maintained unchanged to the [greatest] extent possible.

12. At the same time as the representatives of the estates or *zemstvos,* there shall be invited to membership in the Council of State a few members of the high clergy, but only by direct appointment of the Sovereign.

A few questions arise with respect to the manner in which Your Majesty's sovereign will is to be announced:

I. Will it please Your Majesty to make public all the basic principles of the future participation of representatives of estates or *zemstvos* in affairs of government, or will He confine Himself to a short statement of the basic idea of this participation by indicating in brief the areas which will be affected by it and by observing in a general way that the details are to be worked out subsequently? The latter course seems to be preferable.

II. Will it please Your Majesty to announce that the calling of representatives must be preceded by the organization of *zemstvo* institutions? This seems indispensable. Concurrently one might make public the Sovereign's will that the Council of State take up without delay the examination of the projects concerning these institutions and that their implementation be undertaken immediately.

III. Will it please Your Majesty to order that advance mention be made of some measures which are to be submitted for the consideration of the new membership of the reorganized Council of State, for example, a review of the regulations concerning foreign creeds? Such a declaration has its inconveniences, but it also offers some advantages, among others, with regard to the Western Region and to its Latin population,[6] and also with respect to the general impression such a declaration would produce in Europe.

IV. Will it please Your Majesty to endow the official act announcing Your will with great or little solemnity? In the first case, the act should take the form of a Manifesto. In the second, which appears to be preferable, the announcement may be limited to a Sovereign Decree or Rescript issued to the President of the Council of State or the Minister of the Interior, for by virtue of their office both will be called upon to work most directly and closely on this matter. The form of a decree seems preferable to that of a rescript.

Prior to the drafting of the text of the Decree, Rescript, or Manifesto, it will be necessary to obtain Your Majesty's sovereign instructions with respect to all these questions.

## Explanatory Note to the Project of a New Statute of the Council of State[7]

1. The inviolability of the sovereign rights of the Supreme Power had to be respected in full. In drafting the project this was done in such a way that there was no need even for any qualifying, explanatory, or confirming statement with respect to the inviolability of these rights.

2. The new organization of the Council of State had to be correlated with the existing one as much as possible, in order to squash decisively any suggestion that the proposed transformation

---

[6] The Roman Catholic population of the former Polish and Lithuanian territories.

[7] Valuev presented the draft proposal of a new statute for the Council of State on November 18, 1863, accompanied by a statement explaining the basic principles on which the draft was based and which had been approved by the Emperor on April 15, 1863.

would substantially broaden the rights and powers of the Council of State.

3. Measures had to be taken to prevent the new element introduced to participate in the Council of State from acquiring a dominant influence in it. The consultative character of the new element's participation had to be fully maintained, not only with respect to the supreme governmental authority [that is, the Emperor], but also with respect to the Council of State in its present form. At this point the difficulty arising from the great number of local representatives admitted to the Council of State had to be removed. If [together with the regular Council of State] these representatives constituted a single assembly, then the majority would clearly always be on their side. If on the other hand they constituted a completely separate assembly, there would be two consultative chambers, and the institution's [the Council of State's] unity would be lost. To avoid these inconveniences, the project contains a special arrangement. On the model of the terminology of the statute on the *zemstvo* institutions, the representatives are called "state delegates" [*gosudarstvennyi glasnyi*]. They constitute a special "Congress" [*s'ezd*] which is considered identical in rights to a department of the Council of State, but with this difference: not all its members are invited to the General Assembly [of the Council] (as are all members of a department), but only a specified number of delegates elected for this purpose in every single case. Their number is limited to sixteen, so that in the General Assembly [of the Council] the regular members have a majority of over twice this number. In this way the opinions of the delegates present would be heard and subsequently transmitted for the information of the Monarch, while the conclusions of the whole "Congress" of delegates would be in the manner of an advisory opinion, presented in the same form as the departmental minutes, which can be forwarded to the Monarch for his consideration. Furthermore, it is provided that: the Congress of delegates is in session for specified periods of times, in its absence the normal flow of business does not stop in the Council, and the latter's business is divided into two categories: matters taken up without the participation of the delegates and those with it.

4. Steps had to be taken to prevent the Congress from being carried away by single-minded enthusiasms, and for this reason the

general supervision of the Congress' work had to be entrusted to a person possessing the government's confidence. To this end it was suggested that the chairman be a member of the Council of State, appointed by the Sovereign. Thus the chairman of the Congress would be identical to a chairman of a department of the Council, and the analogy between the departments and the Congress would be fully preserved. The chairman is to be assisted by two elected vice-chairmen. The chancellery of the Congress is not to be separated from the Chancellery of State. A special State Secretary is adjoined to the Congress, but the elective principle is introduced in the persons of three elective secretaries, whose particular duties are defined in the project.

5. Some degree of government influence on the make-up of the Congress had to be secured. To this end it was suggested that, besides the elected delegates, there be a certain number appointed by the government. These would include the so-called *catégories des capacités*.[8] Of course, their number had to be limited, and it was suggested that it not exceed one fifth of the number of elected delegates.

6. Without entering into detailed regulations, the principal rules of procedure for the Congress of Delegates had to be established. These rules are included in the text of the project.

---

[8] Distinguished representatives of scholarship, technology, the arts, the professions, and the business community appointed to participate in a government body or sit in a representative assembly.

# IX

# Memorandum Submitted to the Emperor by the Minister of the Interior, Count M. T. Loris-Melikov (28 January 1881)

———◆———

### Introduction

The proposal submitted by Valuev in 1863 was not acted upon. The situation, as Valuev had predicted, continued to deteriorate; "public opinion" found itself more and more cut off from and in opposition to the government; revolutionary ideologies and radical groups came to dominate the minds of the intelligentsia. In the 1870's the revolutionaries resorted to terrorism in the hope of arousing the alleged latent revolutionary potential of the masses. Sentenced to death by the *Narodnaia Volia* (the most effective of these terrorist groups), Emperor Alexander II, Autocrat of All Russia, became almost a hunted animal.

Called upon to rescue the government from this predicament, General Mikhail Tarielovich Loris-Melikov (1825-88) was appointed head of a Supreme Administrative Commission which managed to break the terrorist wave temporarily.

Loris-Melikov realized quite clearly that this was not enough; what was needed was to restore confidence in the government. In particular it was essential to have the moderately liberal and loyal elements among Russia's educated and economic elite come out openly in support of the regime. This could be achieved, however, only if these moderate elements were given a sense of being in communication with the government, of having their knowledge and ideas taken into consideration in the process of government. If such a common ground could be achieved, if communications could be restored between "society" and the administration, Loris-Melikov believed, there would be no need to fear either the terrorists or the consequences of gradual reform measures.

To this end Loris-Melikov presented a project (known as the "Constitution of Loris-Melikov") which in fact took up Valuev's suggestion of inviting elected select representatives of "public opinion" in a consultative capacity for working out major pieces of legislation. As the reader will notice, Loris-Melikov's proposal was even more modest than Valuev's. It certainly was nothing like a "constitution," and Alexander III's belief that it would be Russia's first step toward constitutionalism and ruin appears, in retrospect, to have been a tragic misconception, both of the plan and of the country's needs.

From "Konstitutsiia grafa Loris-Melikova," Appendix 2,
by Prince N. V. Golitsyn in *Byloe,* No. 10-11
(April-May, 1918), book 4-5, pp. 162-66.

[On top of the original in Alexander III's hand: "Thank God that this criminal and hasty step toward constitution was not taken, and that this whole fantastic project was rejected by quite an insignificant minority in the Council of Ministers—A."]

In February of last year Your Majesty deigned to entrust me with the duties of Chief of the Supreme Administrative Commission [*verkhovnaia rasporiaditel'naia komissiia*], set up for the preservation of order in the state and the restoration of social peace. Then, in August of the same year, after abolishing the Supreme Administrative Commission, Your Majesty deigned to call me to the Ministry of the Interior, which is concerned with the safeguard of order in the state. Entrusting me with such a heavy obligation at a time difficult for Russia, Your Majesty deigned to instruct me that, for the sake of the success of the task with which I was charged, it was necessary not only to take measures for strictly preventing the manifestations of harmful social teachings and for firmly consolidating the government's authority (temporarily shaken by the regrettable events of the last years), but primarily also to give possible satisfaction to the lawful needs and requirements of the population. From that time on, acting in the sense indicated by Your Majesty merely as the strict executor of Your designs, Sire, I may now assure Your Majesty that the first steps along the path traced by Your Sovereign will have already had a noticeable benefit: the gradual return of public life to its normal course satisfies, to a considerable degree, the aspirations of a large segment of the loyal elements of society and strengthens the population's confidence, temporarily shaken, in the force and solidity of the government's authority in Russia. The coordinated actions of the institutions of the state in protecting public and social order; the alleviation in the condition of those exiled by administrative decree, especially among the student youth; a more sympathetic attitude brought to the Empire's educational policies; greater attention paid by the government to local *zemstvo* needs in the broadest sense, as expressed by favorable action on petitions that had previously been left unanswered and by senatorial inspections whose main purpose is to study these needs; the abolition of the salt tax hated by the people; review of the press legislation [censorship laws], which has not accomplished its aim—all these steps have had and are still having a beneficial impact on society in that they calm its excitement and arouse its readiness to serve You, Sire, loyally and with all their strength in completing the great task of the state's reforms which You have initiated from the very first days of Your accession to the throne of Your ancestors.

I take the liberty of reporting most dutifully to Your Majesty that it is essential to take advantage of this mood to consolidate public order more firmly. As a result of events which occurred along with, but were not caused by, the appearance of false social teachings, the great reforms of Your Majesty's reign seem at the present time partly incomplete and partly uncoordinated. Moreover, many questions of prime importance to the state, long since decided by Your sovereign will, lie without action in the chancelleries of various institutions. To complete the reforms and to solve the questions on the agenda, much information is already available in the offices of the central administration—information acquired through experience over the past years and gathered through the activities of senatorial inspections. As the latter had as their primary aim to investigate the actual conditions in the provinces and the local needs, they ought to contribute much to this information and to the clarification, on the basis of local data, of the direction which must be imparted to the future reform activities of the central institutions in order to secure their success. But even if fully analyzed, this information will no doubt prove inadequate in the absence of practical advice from persons intimately acquainted with local conditions and needs.

In view of what has been stated above, it is impossible, in my opinion, not to be struck by the thought that the necessary and effective way of continuing the struggle against sedition consists precisely in calling upon society to participate in the elaboration of the measures needed at the present time. Only the manner of putting this idea into effect is of basic importance and can be the subject of serious discussion.

Turning to a search for the proper procedure, first of all I have to state to Your Majesty my profound conviction that for Russia it is impossible to organize popular representation in imitation of Western patterns; not only are these alien to the Russian people, but they even could shake its basic political outlook and introduce troubles whose consequences are difficult to foresee. Similarly, the proposal put forth by some adherents of the ancient institutions of the Russian state, of establishing a *Zemskaia Duma* or a *Zemskii Sobor* seems to me far from opportune. Changed notions and changed relationships between the constituent parts of the Russian state, as well as the latter's present geographic limits, have removed us so far from the times of these ancient forms of representation that a mere reproduction of the ancient pattern of representation would be difficult to implement, and in any case a dangerous experiment of a return to the past.

In view of the opinions expressed in some quarters of society regarding the necessity of taking recourse to representative institutions for the sake of maintaining order in Russia, and in recognition of the fact that these opinions are only expressive of the need that has developed to serve the common weal, I believe that the most practical means for giving a lawful expression for this need lies along the already tested lines laid down at Your Majesty's wise direction in working out the peasant reform. Of course, it will be necessary to adjust this procedure to the needs and tasks of today.

Based on this fundamental point of departure, and taking into consideration that there already exist on-the-spot, permanent institutions capable of giving information and conclusions on questions to be discussed by the central government, it seems to me desirable to establish in St. Petersburg temporary Preparatory Commissions, on the model of the editorial commissions organized in 1858, so that the labors of these commissions can be examined with the help of representatives of the *zemstvos* and of some major cities.[1]

In every case, the Sovereign's directive would prescribe the composition of these Preparatory Commissions, which would consist of representatives of central government institutions, and to them would be invited, with the Sovereign's consent, informed and loyal persons, in government service and outside it, known for their special scholary work or for their experience in one or another area of government administration or public life.

The chairman should be a person endowed with the Sovereign's trust [and should be] chosen from high government officials. Inspecting senators, upon completion of their inspections, will also become members of the commissions.

---

[1] This refers to the procedure by which the Emancipation Act of 1861 had been drafted. A special, secret Main Committee of a few influential dignitaries worked out the basic principles of the emancipation. Provincial Commissions were set up in every province; they consisted of elected and appointed members and had to present draft proposals for an emancipation settlement based on local conditions. The projects worked out by the Provincial Commissions were forwarded to an Editorial Commission in St. Petersburg that was subdivided into several sections (administration, economy, justice). The sections of the Editorial Commission called in representatives of the nobility from the provinces to clarify problems arising from special local conditions and situations.

At first, the number of the commissions should be limited to two, in accordance with the major areas of their activity; administrative-economic and financial. Each commission could be subdivided into sections or subcommissions. The administrative-economic commission could concern itself with the following subjects within the jurisdiction of the Ministry of the Interior (they could be taken up either at the same time or singly in order):

(a) Reform of the local provincial administration, in order to define precisely its rights and duties and to coordinate the administrative needs and institutions with those of justice and public welfare.

(b) On the basis of experience, make additions to the statute of [Emancipation of] 19 February 1861 and subsequent regulations concerning the peasantry, so that they correspond to the ascertained needs of the peasant population.

(c) Devise means to: (i) bring a rapid end to the obligations that former peasant-serfs still have toward their [former] owners; (ii) alleviate redemption payments in those areas where experience has shown them to be particularly burdensome.

(d) To review the statutes of the *zemstvo* and towns in order to correct and complement them in line with previous directives.

(e) Organization of foodstuff supplies and of the public supply system in general.

(f) Measures to protect cattle breeding.

The subjects for the activity of the financial commission (taxes, passports, etc.) would have to be defined by Your Majesty on the basis of a report by the Minister of Finance, after consultation with the Minister of the Interior, since many of the matters within the areas of competence of these two ministries are closely related to each other.

The commissions would have the obligation to draft law projects within the limits set by Your sovereign will.

At the direction of the Supreme Power the law projects drafted by the Preparatory Commissions would be presented to a *General Commission* to be set up under the chairmanship of a person specially designated by Your sovereign will; its membership would consist of the chairman and members of the Preparatory Commissions, and there also would be added elected representatives from the provinces where the *zemstvo* institutions have been in-troduced, as well as from a few important cities, at the rate of two from every province and city. To attract genuinely useful and knowledgeable persons, the provincial *zemstvo* assemblies and city councils [*gorodskaia duma*] would have the right to elect not only their own delegate but also other persons from the population of the province or city.

From those provinces where *zemstvo* institutions have not yet been established, delegates designated by the local authorities could be invited.

A period of no more than two months could be set for the session of the General Commission.

Draft legislation reviewed and approved or corrected by the General Commission would be submitted to the Council of State along with the opinions of the competent ministers; moreover, to facilitate the work of the Council of State, Your Majesty may deign to order that a few—ten to fifteen—representatives of public institutions who have demonstrated their special knowledge and experience and outstanding abilities be invited to the Council with right to a vote.

Not only the activities of the Preparatory [Commission] but also those of the General Commission ought to have an exclusively consultative character, which in no way changes the existing order for initiating and considering legislative matters in the Council of State.

The procedure for the preliminary elaboration of the most im-portant questions touching on the life of the nation, as set forth above and already successfully tested, has nothing in common with Western constitutional forms. The Sovereign Power retains fully and exclusively the right to introduce legislative matters at the time and within the limits which it deems desirable.

The drafting of new law proposals by the Preparatory Com-missions, consisting of government officials with the participation of only a few outside persons particularly well known to the gov-ernment, will precede the convocation of members elected by public institutions. All the members of the Preparatory Commis-sions will have membership in the General Commission, and they will explain and support the law projects that have been drafted.

This will be the [particular] duty of the chairmen of the Preparatory Commissions in their capacity as assistants to the chairman of the General Commission.

The composition of the General Commission will be decreed by Your sovereign will in every instance; moreover, the Commission will have the right to work only on matters presented for its consideration.

But before final implementation of all the proposals described above, it would seem to me essential to order now that all the materials which are to be found at present in the departments and other central offices and which are relevant to the problems enumerated earlier that will be discussed in the Preparatory Commissions be collected and ordered according to some system and grouped by subject matter. In every single institution this assignment should be entrusted to the most able and efficient officials, and, if the heads of these institutions so desire, they could also for this preliminary work invite the participation of outsiders who, by virtue of their experience and technical knowledge, could contribute to the success of the assignment. A time limit should be set for the completion of this task, to coincide with the completion of the senatorial inspections; and every single institution, independently of the collection and arrangement of the information at its disposal, could be given authority to transmit to the Preparatory Commissions the results of its labors, not merely in the form of raw documentation but also in the form of draft proposals of law projects based on them. On the basis of an approximate estimate, this preliminary work—i.e., processing the materials and projects submitted by both the institutions and the inspecting senators—could be completed by the Fall of this year and forwarded to the Preparatory Commissions. The latter's activity should be conducted in such a way that the General Commission, with participation of public representatives, could be called at the beginning of next year after adjournment of the provincial *zemstvo* assemblies.

In the meantime such a program could give a proper outlet to the noticeable striving of the elements of society to be of service to throne and country; and this surely will bring to the life of the nation an invigorating element and afford the government an opportunity of making use of the experience of local leaders who are closer to the life of the people than the officials of central administrations.

These considerations, together with the excitement created among the loyal elements of society by the joyous expectation of the further development of the reforms undertaken by Your Imperial Majesty, cannot fail to deserve serious attention. I dare to express, Sire, my profound conviction that failure to satisfy these expectations will unfailingly produce perhaps not a complete cooling, but at least an indifference to the public weal; and as the sad experience of recent years has shown, such a situation offers the most fertile ground for the propaganda of anarchy.

If Your Imperial Majesty deigns to share the ideas expressed by me, would it please Your Majesty, after approving the propositions set forth in this memorandum, to order that the examination of ways to implement them be entrusted to several persons of Your Imperial Majesty's choosing.

*Adjutant-General,* COUNT LORIS-MELIKOV

28 January 1881, St. Petersburg

# X

## All-Highest Manifesto
## on the Establishment of a State Duma

### Introduction

When in April, 1881, Alexander III rejected the proposal of Loris-Melikov, all hopes of establishing rapport between the government and the enlightened part of public opinion vanished. The death of Alexander III did not change the situation, as Nicholas II in 1894 bluntly turned down a suggestion for establishing such "contacts" as "senseless dreams." But the events of 1900-1904 were to prove that Nicholas's statement was not the autocracy's last word. Political terrorism, peasant unrest, large-scale industrial strikes, and the frustration and bitterness generated by the defeats and losses of the Russo-Japanese War combined to bring about a truly revolutionary situation by the summer of 1905.

The newly appointed Minister of the Interior, A. G. Bulygin, persuaded the Emperor to grant a limited constitution. In fact, however, what he suggested was rather an extension of Valuev's proposal than a genuine constitution. Though given full recognition as part of the legislative power in the state, the representatives were to be elected by a very narrow electorate and allotted very limited functions. As it was, the proposal had come too late and offered too little to satisfy the aroused nation. Without having been given a try, Bulygin's project was abandoned, and, driven to the wall by the general strike of October, 1905, Nicholas II promised to convene a *duma* elected on the basis of well-nigh universal male suffrage. Bulygin's project turned out to have been the last attempt by the autocracy to reform itself without losing its basic character.

From *Sobranie uzakonenii i rasporiazhenii pravitel'stva,*
*izdavaemoe pri Pravitel'stvennom Senate*
(6 August 1905), No. 141, Section I, Vol. 2,
article 1325, pp. 1967-2007.

By the Grace of God, We, Nicholas the Second, Emperor and Autocrat of All Russia, King of Poland, Grand Duke of Finland, etc., etc., etc., We do make it known to all Our loyal subjects:

The Russian state has been created and has waxed strong through the unbroken union of Tsar and people, of people and Tsar. The concord and union prevailing between the Tsar and people are the great moral force which over the course of centuries has shaped Russia, has protected it against all misfortunes and disasters, and is to this day a pledge to its unity, independence and security, to its material prosperity, and its spiritual progress, both present and future.

In Our manifesto of 26 February 1903 [1] We appealed to all loyal sons of the Fatherland to band together in order to perfect the system of government through the establishment of a solid system of local administration. Even at that time We [entertained] the idea of coordinating the elected public institutions with government authorities and of eradicating the discord existing among

---

[1] See *Sobranie uzakonenii i rasporiazhenii pravitel'stva* (1903), Section I, Part 1, No. 20, article 246, pp. 471-73 ("O prednachertaniiakh k usovershenstvovaniiu gosudarstvennogo poriadka"—On the guidelines for the improvement of the system of government). The manifesto made vague promises to work for legislation to improve the condition of the peasantry and of the economy.

them, a discord which has such a harmful effect on the normal life of the state. Our Predecessors, the Autocratic Tsars, also never ceased thinking about this problem.

Following their good beginnings, the time has now come to summon elected men from all the Russian lands to permanent and active participation in the making of laws, and to this end add to the existing highest governmental institutions a special consultative legislative establishment which will be entrusted with the preliminary elaboration and consideration of law projects and with the examination of state revenues and expenditures.

Wherefore, leaving intact the fundamental law of the Russian Empire[2] as it refers to the existence of the Autocratic Power, We have deemed it desirable to establish a State Duma and to approve its electoral statute, applying these laws to the whole Empire, except for those changes that will be necessary in the case of a few border regions with special conditions.

With regard to the participation in the State Duma of elected representatives from the Grand Duchy of Finland on legislative matters of interest to both the Empire and the Grand Duchy, We shall decree separately.

At the same time We have also ordered the Minister of the Interior to submit without delay for Our approval the rules for implementing the electoral statute to the State Duma, so that the members from fifty provinces and the Region of the Cossack Host of the Don may present themselves at the Duma not later than the middle of January, 1906.

We reserve for Ourselves all concern for the further improvement of the statute of the State Duma; and when experience itself will show the necessity of making changes in the statute to satisfy best the needs of the times and the welfare of the state, We shall not fail to issue the appropriate directives in due course.

We are confident that the men whom the confidence of the entire population has elected and who now are called to work on

---

[2] Articles defining the nature of the sovereign power in Book I, Volume 1, of the *Svod Zakonov* ("Digest" of Laws), which came into force on January 1, 1835. For a discussion of the nature of the fundamental laws, see B. E. Nol'de, "Zakony osnovnye v russkom prave" (Fundamental Laws in Russian Law), *Pravo* (1913), Nos. 8-9, pp. 447-61 and 524-41.

legislation jointly with the Government will prove themselves before all of Russia worthy of the Imperial trust which summons them to this great task, and that, in full accord with the other institutions of the state and the authorities established by Us, they will usefully and zealously help Us in Our labors for the good of Our common Mother Russia, for the unity, security, and greatness of the state, and the peace and prosperity of the people.

Calling God's blessings on the labors of the state institution established by Us, with unshakable faith in God's mercy and in the irrevocability of the great historical destiny Divine Providence has ordained for our dear Fatherland, We firmly hope that with the help of Almighty God and the unanimous efforts of its sons Russia will emerge in triumph from its present difficult trials and that it will be reborn with the power, greatness, and glory which a thousand years of history have imprinted on it.

*Given in Peterhof, the sixth day of August,*
*in the 1905th year of the birth of Our Lord*
*and the eleventh of Our reign.*
NICHOLAS

### Statute of the State Duma

1. The State Duma is established for the preliminary elaboration and discussion of legislative proposals which are submitted, by virtue of the Fundamental Laws, through the Council of State to the Supreme Autocratic Power.

2. The State Duma is composed of members elected by the population of the Russian Empire for five years according to the rules set forth in the electoral statute of the Duma.

3. The State Duma may be dissolved by decree of His Imperial Majesty prior to the expiration of its five-year term (article 2). The same decree orders new elections to the Duma.

4. The duration of the yearly sessions of the State Duma and the periods of adjournment are set by decree of His Imperial Majesty.

5. The State Duma is organized in a General Assembly and in Committees. . . .

7. The following quorums are required for lawful sessions of the State Duma: for the General Assembly, no less than one third of all members of the State Duma; for a Committee, no less than one half of its members.

8. The expenses connected with the upkeep of the State Duma are borne by the State Treasury. . . .

10. The President of the State Duma submits reports on the Duma's activities for Imperial consideration. . . .

14. Members of the State Duma enjoy complete freedom of judgment and opinion on questions pertaining to the Duma's competence and are not accountable to their electors.

15. A member of the State Duma may not be deprived or restricted in his freedom except by order of a judicial authority; nor may he be personally detained for debts. . . .

17. A member of the State Duma loses his status in case of: (a) loss of Russian citizenship, (b) entrance into active military service, (c) appointment to a salaried position in the government service, (d) loss of the qualifications for participation in the election. . . .

20. For criminal deeds committed in the execution or because of the execution of the obligation appertaining to their status, members of the State Duma are called to account according to the rules and procedures provided for the case when members of the Council of State violate the duties of their office. . . .

24. Ministers and Heads of separate departments[3] do not have a seat in the State Duma, but they may attend its sessions and give clarifications personally or through their deputies, or through the chiefs or assistant chiefs of particular divisions of the central administration, or through officials delegated by Ministers and department Heads.

25. The Ministers and Heads of separate departments are under obligation to give the explanations as set forth in article 24 if the State Duma, its General Assembly, or any one of its committees will deem such an explanation necessary. . . .

---

[3] Separate departments were administrative offices of status equal to that of the Ministries, set up to deal with special and technical problems (transportation, peasant settlement, etc.).

33. The following belong to the State Duma's area of competence:

(a) all matters requiring the promulgation of laws and the creation of staffs, as well as changes, additions, suspensions, and abrogations therein;

(b) budgets of the ministries, the chief administrations, and the state, as well as Treasury appropriations not foreseen in the budget. . . ;

(c) the State Comptroller's account of the implementation of the state budget;

(d) alienation of state revenues or property requiring Imperial sanction;

(e) matters concerning the building of railroads on direct order and at the expense of the Treasury;

(f) acts of incorporation involving exceptions to existing legislation;

(g) matters submitted for the State Duma's consideration by special Imperial command.

34. The State Duma is given the right to initiate proposals to abrogate or amend existing laws or to promulgate new ones. But these proposals may not touch upon the principles of the organization of the state as set forth in the Fundamental Laws.

35. Ministers and Heads of separate departments under the jurisdiction of the Governing Senate may be required by the State Duma to provide information and explanations concerning the actions of Ministers, Heads of departments, or their subordinate officials and institutions which in the opinion of the Duma violate existing legislation.

36. Matters to be considered by the State Duma are introduced by the Ministers, Heads of separate departments, and also by the State Secretary.

37. Matters introduced into the State Duma are first discussed in its committees and then submitted for consideration to its General Assembly. . . .

41. Outsiders are not admitted to the sessions of the General Assembly of the State Duma or of its committees.

42. The President of the Duma may grant to representatives of the press permission to attend sessions of the General Assembly

(except closed sessions), but not to more than one representative from a single publication. . . .

44. Minutes of all sessions of the General Assembly of the State Duma are drafted by official stenographers, and, after being approved by the President of the Duma, they are made public in the press (except for the minutes of closed sessions). . . .

46. A Minister or Head of department may at any stage of the proceedings withdraw any matter he has submitted to the State Duma. But matters under consideration as a result of a legislative question having been raised in the Duma (article 34) may be withdrawn by the Minister or Head of department only with the consent of the Duma's General Assembly.

47. The opinion approved (adopted) by the majority of members of the General Assembly of the Duma is viewed as concluding consideration by the State Duma. This conclusion must indicate clearly the Duma's approval or disapproval of the proposals submitted to it. The changes suggested by the Duma must be indicated in clearly expressed statements.

48. Legislative proposals considered by the State Duma are submitted, with its conclusions, to the Council of State. Upon examination in the Council (except in the case indicated in article 49), they are submitted to His Imperial Majesty's approval, together with the Duma's recommendations, following the procedures set forth in the statute of the Council of State.

49. Legislative proposals rejected by a two-thirds majority of the General Assemblies of both the State Duma and the Council of State are returned to the appropriate Minister or Head of department for further consideration and, with His Imperial Majesty's permission, renewed submittal for legislative action.

50. In those instances when the Council of State encounters difficulties in accepting the conclusions of the State Duma, by resolution of the General Assembly of the Council of State the matter may be submitted, in order to reconcile the opinions of the State Duma and Council of State, to a committee consisting of an equal number of members from each institution, elected by the General Assemblies of the Council and the Duma. The chairman of such a committee is either the President of the Council of State or the chairman of one of its departments. . . .

52, 53.//If there is no quorum or too great a delay in the State Duma, a business matter may be referred by Imperial order to the Council of State without the Duma's opinion.//

54. To amend or abrogate existing or new legislation, members of the State Duma submit a written statement to the President of the Duma. The statement must be accompanied by a draft project of the basic changes proposed, together with an explanatory memorandum. If this statement is signed by no less than thirty members, the President submits it for consideration to the appropriate committee.

55.//Ministers and other appropriate officials must be informed of the date when the amendment or abrogation of legislation will be up for consideration in the Duma; they must be furnished with copies of the statements mentioned in article 54 no less than one month prior to session.//. . .

57. If a Minister or Head of a separate department or State Secretary does not share the considerations offered in favor of amending or abrogating existing or new legislation that have been approved both by the committee and a two-thirds majority of the members of the General Assembly of the State Duma, the President of the Duma submits the matter to the Council of State, through which it goes up to His Imperial Majesty's consideration according to established procedure. In case His Majesty orders legislative action, the task of detailed elaboration is entrusted to the appropriate Minister or Head of a separate department or to the State Secretary.

58. Members of the State Duma may submit statements in writing to the President of the Duma if they wish information or an explanation concerning actions by Ministers, chiefs of main administrations, and their subordinate officials and institutions which are considered to have violated existing legislation. These statements must indicate what law is considered to have been violated and what the violation consisted of. If the statement is signed by no less than thirty members, the President of the Duma submits it for discussion to the General Assembly of the Duma.

59.//If adopted by a majority of the General Assembly, the statement referred to under article 58 is communicated to the Minister or Head of department concerned.//

60.//Minister or Head of department must inform the Duma within one month why he cannot fulfill its demand for information and explanation.//

61. If by a two-thirds majority the General Assembly of the State Duma does not accept the communication of the Minister or Head of department as satisfactory, the matter is submitted through the Council of State to His Majesty's consideration.

### Electoral Statute

1. Elections to the State Duma take place (a) in the provinces and regions, (b) in the following cities: St. Petersburg and Moscow, as well as Astrakhan, Baku, Warsaw, Vil'no, Voronezh, Ekaterinoslav, Irkutsk, Kazan, Kiev, Kishinev, Kursk, Lodz, Nizhnii-Novgorod, Odessa, Orel, Riga, Rostov-on-the-Don, together with Nakhichevan, Samara, Saratov, Tashkent, Tiflis, Tua, Kharkav, Iaroslavl. *Note:* Elections to the State Duma from the provinces of the Kingdom of Poland, from the regions of the Ural and of Tugaisk, from the provinces and regions of Siberia, from the Governor-Generalships of the Steppes and of Turkestan, and from the Viceroyalty of the Caucasus, as well as elections by nomadic natives, will be conducted according to special rules.

2. The number of members of the State Duma from each province, region, and town is set forth in the roster appended.

3. The election of members of the State Duma from the provinces and regions (article 1) is performed by provincial electoral assemblies. These assemblies, under the chairmanship of the provincial marshals of the nobility (or their substitutes), are composed of electors chosen by the following assemblies: (a) of landowners in the districts, (b) of electors from the cities, (c) of authorized representatives of the townships [*volost'*] and Cossack villages [*stanitsa*].

4.//The number and distribution of electors for each region, district, and township are given in the attached roster.//. . .

6. The following do not participate in the elections: (a) persons of the female sex, (b) persons under twenty-five years of age, (c) students in educational institutions, (d) military ranks of

army and navy on active duty, (e) nomadic natives, (f) foreign subjects. . . .

8. [These also] do not participate in elections: (a) governors and vice-governors, as well as governors of cities[4] and their assistants, within the borders of the territory under their jurisdiction, and (b) persons exercising police functions in the provinces and towns where the elections take place. . . .

12. In the assemblies of landowners of the district participate: (a) persons owning, or holding in possession for life, land subject to *zemstvo* dues in the [minimum] amount set forth for each district in the roster appended; (b) persons possessing mining grants in the district, in the [minimum] amount set forth in the roster; (c) persons holding in full property or as possession for life—besides land—real property in the district (exclusive of commercial and industrial enterprises) evaluated by the *zemstvo* at not less than 15,000 rubles; (d) agents of persons owning in the district either not less than one tenth of the amount of land set forth in the aforementioned roster, or other real property (see section b above) evaluated at no less than 1,500 rubles; and (e) agents of clergy owning land in the district. . . .

16. In the assemblies of city electors participate: (a) persons holding within the city limits, in full property or in possession for life, real estate either assessed for purposes of *zemstvo* taxes at no less than 1,500 rubles or requiring a business license as a commercial or industrial enterprise: if it is a commercial enterprise, a certificate of the first two categories, if it is an industrial enterprise a certificate of the first five categories, and if it is a navigational enterprise, the payment of a business tax of not less than 50 rubles per year; (b) persons paying within the limits of urban settlements a state rent tax of the tenth category or higher; (c) persons paying within the limits of the city and its district a basic business tax of the first category on individual business activities; and (d) persons owning in the district commercial/industrial enterprises as defined in section a of the present article.

17. In the electoral assembly of representatives from townships [*volost'*] participate two delegates elected from each town-

---

[4] *Gradonachal'nik:* appointed official in charge of the police of larger cities.

ship assembly in the district. These delegates are elected by township assemblies from among qualified peasants belonging to the village communes of the township. . . .

19. In the cities listed in article 1, b, the following may participate in electoral assemblies: (a) persons holding within the city limits, in full property or in possession for life, real estate assessed for purposes of city taxes at no less than 3,000 rubles in the capitals, and at no less than 1,500 rubles in the other cities; (b) persons owning within the city limits of the capitals a commercial establishment of the first category or an industrial establishment of the first three categories, or a shipping enterprise paying a basic business tax of not less than 500 rubles a year; or [persons owning within the city limits of] the other cities: commercial enterprises of the first two categories, industrial enterprises of the first five categories, or a shipping enterprise paying a basic business tax of not less than 50 rubles per annum; (c) persons paying within the city limits a basic business tax of the first category for individual business activities; and (d) persons paying within the city limits a state rent tax of the tenth category or higher.

21.//For purposes of the electoral franchise, persons holding property in common are credited with their own share of the property.//. . .

40. Elections of electoral assemblies are by secret vote with the use of voting spheres;[5] election to the city electoral assemblies are by secret written ballot. . . .

47.//Right to register complaints against irregularities.//. . .

49. In every provincial electoral assembly the electors from the assemblies of delegates of [rural] townships first elect one member of the State Duma from among their ranks. Then the electoral assembly as a whole elects the remaining members (as per roster in article 2) of the Duma from all the qualified electors. The election is secret by means of voting spheres.

50. City electoral assemblies (article 5) elect from qualified electors the required number of members of the State Duma (article 2) in secret vote by means of spheres. . . .

---

[5] Balloting frequently took place by casting white and black balls; such a method was particularly indicated for a largely illiterate electorate.

53. Only persons who have signified their consent may be elected to membership in the State Duma. Persons holding offices carrying a regular salary in the state civil service must relinquish their post in case of their election to the State Duma. . . .

55. No one ignorant of the Russian language may be elected to the Duma.

# Bibliography

The literature bearing on the problems with which the present volume is concerned is at the same time vast and inadequate. It is vast because before 1917 many sources had been published and a large number of studies written from them. It is inadequate because most of these studies are either antiquated in approach and interpretation or concerned with relatively trivial detail. There is still a dearth of interpretation and synthesis of Russian institutional life during the eighteenth and nineteenth centuries. While the situation is unsatisfactory with respect to works in Russian, it is well-nigh hopeless with regard to the literature available in the major Western languages. True, the *corpus* of monographs and shorter studies on various special aspects of Imperial Russian history has grown rapidly in the last twenty years or so. But in the main the work done so far has not focused on the history of institutions and administration, but rather on ideas, ideologies, and the revolutionary movement.

As the reading knowledge of Russian spreads rapidly in the academic community, it becomes possible to supplement the rather short list of works in Western languages (and many important problems and periods are not represented on this list) with a sample of the relevant literature available in Russian.

Helpful indications of the recent literature in the field (from which one can work backward to older studies) may be found in the folllowing bibliographical repertories: David Shapiro, *A Select Bibliography of Works in English on Russian History 1801-1917*, Oxford: B. Blackwell, 1962; H. Jablonowski and W. Philipp, eds., *Forschungen zur Osteuropäischen Geschichte*, Vols. I, III, IV, V, VII, Wiesbaden: O. Harassowitz, 1954-59; as well as the issues of the *American Bibliography of Slavic and East European Studies* published since 1957 by the University of Indiana Press. For Russian reference material, see in particular: *Bibliografiia russkoi bibliografii po istorii SSSR* (Annotirovannyi perechen' bibliograficheskikh ukazatelei izdannykh do 1917 goda), Moscow: 1957; and *Istoriia SSSR— Ukazatel' sovetskoi literatury 1917-1952*, 2 vols. (and 2 vols. of indices), Moscow: 1956-58.

1. Basic information and traditional interpretations of Russia's institutional and administrative history from Peter the Great to the revolution of 1905 are found in the general histories of Russian public law. Among these by far the best is N. M. Korkunov, *Russkoe gosudarstvennoe pravo*, 4th ed., 2 vols., St. Petersburg: 1901. A readable and useful survey of the same material but along strictly historical lines is G. V. Vernadskii, *Ocherk istorii prava russkogo gosudarstva XVIII-XIX vv.*, Prague: 1924. The Soviet approach and interpretation can be found in S. V. Iushkov, *Istoriia gosudarstva i prava SSSR*, Part I, Moscow: 1950. Lothar Schultz, *Russische Rechtsgeschichte*, Lahr: Moritz Schauenburg, 1951, is the only survey in a Western language. For a brief discussion of the major institutions from the point of view of a liberal at the end of the nineteenth century see Maxim Kovalevsky, *Russian Political Institutions*, Chicago: University of Chicago Press, 1902. Anatole Leroy-Beaulieu, *L'Empire des Tsars et les russes*, 4th revised ed., Vol. II, Paris: 1898, is not only a classic but also one of the most perceptive analyses of the institutional scene in the second half of the nineteenth century. A comprehensive study and guide to Russian imperial institutions is announced for publication in late 1965 by Erik Amburger in the series *Studien zur Geschichte Osteuropas*, Leiden: E. J. Brill, Publishers.

2. There is no satisfactory general history of reform efforts, and the following are only first steps in this direction: V. E. Iakushkin, *Gosudarstvennaia vlast' i proekty gosudarstvennoi reformy v Rossii*, St. Petersburg: 1906; S. Swatikow, *Die Entwürfe der Änderung der russischen Reichsverfassung*, Heidelberg: 1904. The important studies of V. I. Semevskii are too numerous to be listed here; see the bibliography of his works in *Golos Minuvshego*, No. 10, 1916.

3. There is a large body of source materials and studies of the major administrative institutions of Imperial Russia in addition to the basic information provided by the works cited in paragraph 1. The classic interpretative analysis of eighteenth-century administration along legal lines is

A. D. Gradovskii, "Vysshaia administratsiia Rossii XVIII stoletiia i general prokurory," in *Sobranie Sochinenii A. D. Gradovskogo,* Vol. I, St. Petersburg: 1899, pp. 37-297. On the Supreme Privy Council consult B. L. Viazemskii, *Verkhovnyi Tainyi Sovet,* St. Petersburg: 1909. On the Senate there is, first of all, the jubileum history edited by S. F. Platonov, *Istoriia Pravitel'stvuiushchego Senata za dvesti let,* St. Petersburg: 1911. For a detailed study of the Senate in its period of decline after the death of Peter the Great see A. N. Filippov, *Pravitel'stvuiushchii Senat pri Petre Velikom i ego blizhaishikh preemnikakh 1711-1741,* St. Petersburg: 1911 (originally in the *Trudy Iur'evskogo Universiteta,* Iur'ev/Dorpat: 1895, under the title "Istoriia Senata v pravlenii Verkhovnogo Tainogo Soveta i Kabineta"). On the Cabinet of Ministers under Anne see V. Stroev, *Bironovshchina i Kabinet Ministrov,* St. Petersburg: 1909-10. For a discussion of the legal position of the Council of Ministers in the nineteenth and early twentieth centuries see B. E. Nol'de, "Soviet Ministrov," in his *Ocherki russkogo gosudarstvennogo prava,* St. Petersburg: 1911, pp. 85-211. The history of the Council of State is treated in the jubileum publication *Gosudarstvennyi Sovet 1801-1901,* St. Petersburg: 1901, and its antecedents and genesis are exhaustively treated in V. G. Shcheglov, *Gosudarstvennyi Sovet v Rossii, v osobennosti v tsarstvovanii Aleksandra I,* Iaroslavl': 1892-96. A brief summary can be found in R. Maurach, *Der russische Reichsrat,* Berlin: 1939.

In connection with the centennial celebrations of the major ministries in 1902, jubileum volumes were published for each one of them; they contain much valuable official information.

The history of the attempts at codification has been the subject of technical and specialized works too numerous to be listed here. The basic monograph for the efforts made in the eighteenth century is V. Latkin, *Zakonodatel'nye komissii v Rossii v XVIII v.,* St. Petersburg: 1887. The intellectual aspects of the codification efforts are discussed by A. Fateev, "K istorii iuridicheskoi obrazovannosti v Rossii," *Uchenye Zapiski, osnovannye russkoi uchebnoi kollegiei v Prage,* Vol. I, fasc. 3, 1924, pp. 129-256, and A. Lappo-Danilevskii, *Sobranie i svod zakonov Rossiiskoi Imperii, sostavlennoi v tsarstvovanii imperatritsy Ekateriny II,* St. Petersburg: 1898 (first appeared in 1897 in *Zhurnal Ministerstva Narodnogo Prosveshcheniia,* Vols. 309, 310, 311, and 314). A summary, description, and bibliography of Speransky's codification appear in M. Raeff, *Michael Speransky, Statesman of Imperial Russia,* The Hague: M. Nijhof, 1957, Chapter XI.

4. The "imperial" character of the modern Russian state, with particular reference to its national, legal, and administrative variety, has not been investigated very much. Extremely valuable, albeit fragmentary, infor-

mation and analysis on the incorporation of several key regions and their administrative status within the Empire can be found in B. Nolde, *La formation de l'Empire russe*, 2 vols., Paris: 1952-53. On the particular case of Siberia see M. Raeff, *Siberia and the Reforms of 1822*, University of Washington: 1956. For an attempt at a more comprehensive sweep see Georg von Rauch, *Russland—Staatliche Einheit und nationale Vielfalt*, München: 1953. The juridical aspect is discussed in B. Nol'de, "Edinstvo i nerazdel'nost' Rossii," in his *Ocherki russkogo gosudarstvennogo prava*, St. Petersburg: 1911, pp. 475-554.

5. On local government and administration there are almost no satisfactory monographs or easily accessible sources and studies. The old study by A. D. Gradovskii, "Istoricheskii ocherk uchrezhdeniia general-gubernatorstv v Rossii," *Russkii Vestnik* (Nov.-Dec., 1869) is still useful. See also I. Blinov, *Gubernatory-istoriko iuridicheskii ocherk*, St. Petersburg: 1905. There is a vast literature on the *zemstvos* after 1864, but it is not relevant in our context.

6. A. Lappo-Danilevsky, "L'idée de l'état et son évolution en Russie depuis les troubles du XVIIe siècle jusqu'aux réformes du XVIIIe," in P. Vinogradoff, ed., *Essays in Legal History*, Oxford: 1913, pp. 356-83, is an introduction to the pre-Petrine conceptions on the state. The Russian monarchy in the eighteenth century as an institution and a concept is described by N. N. Alexeiev, "Beiträge zur Geschichte des russischen Absolutismus im 18. Jahrhundert," *Forschungen zur Osteuropäischen Geschichte*, Vol. VI, Wiesbaden-Berlin: 1958, pp. 7-81. The history of the traditional Russian view of kingship and its evolution since Peter the Great is given by M. Cherniavsky in *Tsar and People—Studies in Russian Myths*, New Haven: Yale University Press, 1961. For the notions commonly held at the end of the eighteenth century concerning the nature of the Russian monarchy see R. Pipes, "Karamzin's Conception of Monarchy," *Harvard Slavic Studies*, Vol. IV, Cambridge, Mass.: 1957, pp. 35-58. I. Ditiatin, "Verkhovnaia vlast' v Rossii v XVIII veke," in his *Stat'i po istorii russkogo prava*, St. Petersburg: 1896, pp. 591-631, and B. B. Glinskii, "K voprosu o titule samoderzhets," *Istoricheskii Vestnik*, No. 131 (1913), pp. 567-603, are useful discussions of some legal aspects of the question.

7. There are only sketchy and fragmentary accounts and discussions of the imperial bureaucracy; most of the details have to be gleaned from dispersed and varied sources, as well as memoirs, letters, and diaries of contemporaries. M. Aleksandrov, *Gosudarstvo, biurokratiia i absoliutizm v istorii Rossii*, St. Petersburg: 1910, is somewhat polemical. I. M. Kataev has gathered interesting and colorful descriptions of the bureaucracy before the reforms of Alexander II in *Doreformennaia biurokratiia po za-*

*piskam, memuaram i literature,* St. Petersburg (no date). See also M. Raeff, "The Russian Autocracy and Its Officials," *Harvard Slavic Studies,* Vol. IV (1957), pp. 77-92; "L'état, le gouvernement et al tradition politique en Russie impériale avant 1861," *Revue d'Histoire Moderne et Contemporaine* (Oct.-Dec., 1962), pp. 296-305; "Staatsdienst, Aussenpolitik, Ideologien—Die Rolle der Institutionen in der geistigen Entwicklung des russischen Adels im 18. Jahrhundert," *Jahrbücher für Geschichte Osteuropas,* Vol. VII (new series), No. 2 (1959), pp. 147-81.

8. Recently there have been published interesting studies and discussions of the transformation of Russian society and institutions from 1861 to 1914. Valuable material on this problem is contained in E. J. Simmons, ed., *Continuity and Change in Russian and Soviet Thought,* Harvard University Press: 1955, and C. E. Black, ed., *The Transformation of Russian Society,* Harvard University Press: 1960. For the economic policies of the government see Th. H. von Laue, *Sergei Witte and the Industrialization of Russia,* New York: Columbia University Press, 1963, and for an account of professional and public associations, J. Walkin, *The Rise of Democracy in Pre-Revolutionary Russia (Political and Social Institutions Under the Last Three Czars),* New York: Frederick A. Praeger, 1962. The *zemstvo* movement in its relationship to the government and the development of political ideas is treated by George Fischer in *Russian Liberalism —From Gentry to Intelligentsia,* Harvard University Press: 1958. For a survey of the literature on the relationship between "public opinion" and the government see M. Raeff, "Some Reflections on Russian Liberalism," *Russian Review,* Vol. XVIII, No. 3 (July, 1959), pp. 218-30.

9. Background information on specific reigns and reform plans dealt with in the present volume is widely scattered; it also varies greatly in quantity and quality from case to case. Listed below are books and articles that could be used as a starting point for further study of particular reigns and events.

(a) On the reign of Peter the Great the best introduction is the very short but most informative and judicious book of B. H. Sumner, *Peter the Great and the Emergence of Russia,* London: English Universities Press, Ltd., 1950. The German study by R. Wittram, *Peter der Grosse— der Eintritt Russlands in die Neuzeit,* Berlin-Göttingen-Heidelberg: 1954, displays similar qualities. The same author has now expanded his short introduction into a two-volume definitive history, *Peter der Erste, Czar und Kaiser in seiner Zeit,* Göttingen: 1964. For a summary of Catherine's administration see O. Hoetzsch, "Catherine II," in *Cambridge Modern History,* Vol. VI, 1909, pp. 657-701, and the articles of A. Kizevetter collected in his *Istoricheskie siluety—liudi i sobytiia,* Berlin: 1931. Useful information and occasional insights can be garnered on the reign of Elizabeth from S. V. Eshevskii "Ocherk tsarstvovaniia Elizavety Petrovny" in his *Sochineniia po russkoi istorii,* Moscow: 1900, pp. 3-160; on Peter III from H. Fleischhacker, "Porträt Peters III," *Jahrbücher für Geschichte Osteuropas,* Vol. V (new series) (1957), pp. 127-89; on Paul I in E. S. Shumigorskii, *Imperator Pavel I—zhizn' i tsarstvovanie,* St. Petersburg: 1907. The standard biographies on Alexander I are by Grand Duc Nicolas Mikhailovitsch, *L'Empereur Alexandre Ier,* 2 vols., St. Petersburg and Paris: 1912, and N. K. Shil'der, *Imperator Aleksandr Pervyi—ego zhizn' i tsartsvovanie,* 4 vols., St. Petersburg: 1904-5. The classic work of Th. Schiemann, *Geschichte Russlands unter Nikolaus I,* 4 vols., Berlin: 1904-19, is somewhat out of date; the first volume covers the reign of Alexander I. The best account of the reign and policies of Nicholas I is M. Polievktov, *Nikolai I—biografiia i obzor tsarstvovaniia,* Moscow: 1918. For a more detailed study of specific aspects of the government of Nicholas I and a modern interpretation of his reign see S. Monas, *The Third Section— Police and Society in Russia Under Nicholas I,* Harvard University Press: 1961, and N. V. Riasanovsky, *Nicholas I and Official Nationality in Russia, 1825-55,* University of California Press: 1959. A summary account of the reign and reforms of Alexander is available in the "Teach Yourself History" series, W. E. Mosse, *Alexander II and the Modernization of Russia,* London: 1958. There are no adequate or comprehensive treatments of the reigns and policies of Alexander III and Nicholas II.

(b) The classic book on the crisis of 1730 is D. A. Korsakov, *Votsarenie imperatritsy Anny Ioannovny,* Kazan': 1880. The best-known interpretation of the crisis is in the article by P. N. Milioukov, "Les hommes d'en haut et la noblesse," in his *Le Mouvement intellectual russe,* Paris: 1918, pp. 5-86 (originally, "Verkhovniki i shliakhetstvo," in his *Iz istorii russkoi intelligentsii,* St. Petersburg: 1903, pp. 1-51). A different interpretation is defended by W. Recke, "Die Verfassungspläne der russischen Oligarchen im Jahre 1730 und die Thronbesteigung der Kaiserin Anna Ivanovna," *Zeitschrift für Osteuropäische Geschichte,* II (1911), pp. 11-64 and 161-203. A more recent summary is found in H. Fleischhacker, "1730. Nachspiel der petrinischen Reform," *Jahrbücher für Geschichte Osteuropas,* Vol. VI (1941), pp. 201-74. See also G. A. Protasov, " 'Konditsii' 1730g. i ikh prodolzhenie," *Uchenye Zapiski, Tambovskii pedagogicheskii institut,* Vol. XV (1957), pp. 215-31. A. Lipski has tried to rehabilitate the reign of Anne in his article "A Re-examination of the 'Dark Era' of Anna Ioannovna," *American Slavic and East European Review,* Vol. XV (Dec., 1956), pp. 477-88.

For Panin's project see N. Chechulin, "Proekt imperatorskogo soveta," *Zhurnal Ministerstva Narodnogo Prosveshcheniia,* No. 292 (1894), pp. 68-87.

For the Charter to the Russian people consult G. Sacke, *Graf A. Voroncov, A. N. Radiscev un der 'Gnadenbrief' für das russische Volk,* Emsdetten: 1939.

A discussion of the major lines of political debate in the reign of Alexander I and an analysis of Speransky's projects may be found in M. Raeff, *Michael Speransky—Statesman of Imperial Russia,* The Hague: M. Nijhoff, 1957. A. V. Predtechenskii, *Ocherki obshchestvenno-politicheskoi istorii Rossii v pervoi chetverti XIX veka,* Moscow-Leningrad: 1957, is a Soviet interpretation backed by a wealth of important source materials. The main features of the Senatorial party and Unofficial Committee orientations in the light of recently published documents are set forth in M. Raeff, "Le climat politique et les projets de réforme dans les premières années du règne d'Alexandre Ier," *Cahiers du Monde Russe et Soviétique,* Vol. II, No. 4 (Oct.-Dec., 1961), pp. 415-32. The genesis and character of Novosil'tsev's plan are most exhaustively analyzed by G. Vernadsky, *La Charte Constitutionnelle de l'Empire russe de l'an 1820,* Paris: 1933.

Outside of the article of P. Shchegolev, "Iz istorii 'konstitutsionnykh veianii v 1879-1881gg," *Byloe,* Vol. I, No. 12 (Dec., 1906), pp. 264-84, there is nothing much of importance on Valuev's project. For the working of the government at this period one may read with profit the diaries of P. A. Valuev edited by P. A. Zaionchkovskii, 2 vols., Moscow: 1961, and *Dnevnik D. A. Miliutina,* 4 vols., Moscow: 1947-50.

N. V. Golitsyn gives the background of Loris-Melikov's plan and the pertinent source materials in "Konstitutsiia grafa Loris-Melikova," *Byloe* (April-May, 1918), pp. 125-86. A comprehensive treatment on the basis of new archival evidence of Loris-Melikov's role in the government has been given by P. Zaionchkovskii, *Krizis samoderzhaviia na rubezhe 1870-1880kh godov,* Moscow: 1964.

P. N. Miliukov puts the Bulygin *Duma* project in its historical perspective in "Gosudarstvennyi akt 6 avgusta 1905 goda," *Pravo,* No. 31 (6 August 1905).

The source publications from which we have drawn the texts of the projects translated in this volume frequently give further information and discussions of the events connected with the particular project.